LENIN'S WILL

Russian Studies Series
Valery Kuvakin, General Editor

GENERAL INTEREST

History of Russian Philosophy, 2 volumes, edited by Valery
    Kuvakin
The Basic Bakunin: Writings 1869-1871, translated and
    edited by Robert M. Cutler
Anton Chekhov: Stories of Women, edited and translated
    by Paula Ross

FROM THE SECRET ARCHIVES
OF THE FORMER SOVIET UNION

Lenin's Will: Falsified and Forbidden, by Yuri Buranov
Out of the Red Shadows: Anti-Semitism in Stalin's Russia,
    by Gennady V. Kostyrchenko (January 1995)
*The Red Army and the Wehrmacht: How the Soviets Mili-
    tarized Germany in 1922-1923 and Paved the Way for
    Fascism*, by Yuri L. Dyakov and Tatyana S. Bushuyeva
    (February 1995)
The Struggle for Power in Russia in 1923, by Valentina P.
    Vilkova (Spring 1995)

LENIN'S WILL

FALSIFIED AND FORBIDDEN

YURI BURANOV

From the Secret Archives of the Former Soviet Union

 Prometheus Books

59 John Glenn Drive
Amherst, New York 14228-2197

Published 1994 by Prometheus Books

98 97 96 95 94   5 4 3 2 1

Library of Congress Cataloging-in-Publication Data

Buranov, Yuri A., 1933–
    Lenin's will : falsified and forbidden : from the secret archives of the former Soviet Union / Yuri Buranov.
        p.   cm.
    Translated from Russian.
    ISBN 0-87975-886-4 (alk. paper)
    1. Lenin, Vladimir Il'ich, 1870–1924—Will. 2. Heads of state—Soviet Union—Biography. 3. Soviet Union—Politics and government—1917–1936. 4. Eastman, Max, 1883–1969. I. Title.
DK254.L445B87   1994
947.084'1'092—dc20
[B]   94-15108
                                                                                CIP
Printed on acid-free paper in the United States of America.

Contents

5

6   LENIN'S WILL

Key to Abbreviations

CC—Central Committee

CCC—Central Control Commission of the Central Committee of the All-Russian Communist Party (Bolshevik)

CLD—Council of Labor and Defense

CP—Communist Party

CPC—Council of People's Commissars

CPSU—Communist Party of the Soviet Union

FCP—French Communist Party

GCP—German Communist Party

NEP—New Economic Policy

RCP(b)—All-Russian Communist Party (Bolshevik), same as the VKP(b)

RCPSMHD—Russian Center for the Preservation and Study of Modern History Documents (Rossiísky Tsentr Khraneniya i Izucheniya Dokumentov Noveísheí Istorii)

RVSR—Military Revolutionary Council of the Russian Republic

SCNE—Supreme Council of the National Economy, same
    as the SEC
SEC—Supreme Economic Council, same as the SCNE
UCP—Ukrainian Communist Party
VKP(b)—All-Russian Communist Party (Bolshevik), same
    as the RCP(b)

Introduction

Numerous publications have been devoted to Vladimir Ilyich Lenin's final dictations, which he gave while seriously ill, from the end of December 1922 through the beginning of March 1923. One of Lenin's most important dictations, in which he gave brief character descriptions of his closest associates, was published in the USSR only in 1956. This record is often called his "last will." However, his wife, Nadezhda Konstantinovna Krupskaya, considered *everything* he dictated during his illness to be his political will. There has been and still is speculation that Lenin's dictations during that period, particularly his will, were later edited and altered by Joseph Stalin. I have found, in the top secret archives of the Central Committee of the Communist Party, one of the original manuscripts, which, I submit, proves that Lenin's works were partly altered. The changes were made so skillfully that, for example, to the end of his life, Lev D. Trotsky never knew he dealt with the edited, not the original, text of the first and most important of Lenin's dictations, that of December 23, 1922. Stalin's art of falsifying and misinformation surprises historians again and again. In this book I present still more evidence of falsification. In the Rossiísky Tsentr Khraneniya i Izucheniya Dokumentov Noveíshei Istorii (Russian Center for the Preservation and Study of Modern History Documents, or RCPSMHD, the former Central Party Archives of the Communist Party of the Soviet Union Central Committee) there is a case specially fabricated by the Vecheka (All-Russia Extraordinary Commission, later the KGB) in June 1918 concerning the assassination of Mikhail Romanov, brother of the last Russian tsar, Nikolaí II. Lenin's documents, as I will show, were falsified even more skillfully.

In the present investigation I mean to reveal the secrets of this falsification and cast some light on the political struggle that raged in Russia in the 1920s around the question of whether or not to publish Lenin's last works. When Lenin was seriously ill and could not control events any more, his Party associates, making use of the situation, hid his last documents from each other, and first and foremost from Trotsky. The struggle around Lenin's will resulted in the development and further flourishing of what Trotsky academically called Stalin's "school" of falsifying. However, the facts below show that Trotsky himself was a very clever and tough player in the acute struggle for power that raged around Lenin's works.

To my mind, Lenin did not mean to write a political will. To the end of his life, he was struggling for his own position and his political line. Even while dying, he was preparing a report for the next Party Congress.

After Lenin's death his report was kept so secret that its last fragments became known to Party members only in 1956, three years after his successor, Stalin, died.

The dying Lenin thought about those who would come to power after him, but he hardly had an intention of turning his report to the Congress into a political will.

This book is based on previously secret archive documents in the former Central Party Archives of the Communist Party of the Soviet Union's Central Committee, to which I had direct access.

One

The Falsification

The mystery of the alteration of Lenin's political will emerged in the days when he began dictating his "Letter to the Congress." It was believed that the dictations Lenin gave toward the end of December 1922 had been misrepresented, but until recently there was no trustworthy evidence to prove this. I believe that such evidence is now available, showing that, on receiving Lenin's dictations from his secretariat, Stalin most likely changed the wording. In one case this can be proved by reference to an original, and heretofore secret, document. The purpose of this book is not only to determine precisely what the rewordings of Lenin's "Letter to the Congress" were, but also to ascertain how the alteration was accomplished.[1]

In 1970 a handwritten sheet was sent from the General

---

1. Readers not intimately familiar with the political history of the Soviet Union in the early 1920s are strongly urged to review Appendix 1, which appears on pages 203–208.

13

Department of the Communist Party of the Soviet Union (CPSU) Central Committee to the Central Party Archives of the Institute of Marxism-Leninism. It was the text that Lenin dictated on December 23, 1922, which became known as the beginning of the "Letter to the Congress." This document is unique in two respects.

It is absolutely clear that all of Lenin's texts relevant to the "Letter to the Congress" cycle were published on the basis of original typescripts.[2] But this newly discovered document is written in the hand of Stalin's wife, Nadezhda Alliluyeva.[3]

---

2. V.I. Lenin, *Polnoe sobranie sochinenii,* tom 45 (*Complete Works,* vol. 45) (Moscow: Izdatelstbo Politicheskoĭ Literatury, 1964), pp. 341–406. This was also published in English translation in V.I. Lenin, *Collected Works,* vol. 36 (Moscow: Progress Publishers, 1966), pp. 593–611.

3. Nadezhda Sergeievna Alliluyeva (1901–1932), as one of Lenin's secretaries, also helped keep his journal (or diary), in addition to taking dictations. It was she who began the journal on November 21, 1922. Her last entry was on December 18, 1922. It is noteworthy that the next entry, dated December 23, 1922 (the same day as Lenin's first installment of his "Letter to the Congress" cycle), was made by another of Lenin's secretaries, M.A. Volodicheva.

[Editor's note: It is also noteworthy that it was M.A. Volodicheva who took credit for taking the December 23 dictation of the "Letter to the Congress," and that it was she who put her initials on the official typed copy. The reader will notice later that in her declaration of December 29, 1922, Lidia Fotieva, Lenin's head secretary, also maintained that it was Volodicheva who took this particular dictation. Nonetheless, the handwriting in the original copy is clearly Alliluyeva's and handwriting experts have confirmed this. Apparently Alliluyeva wrote out the letter in longhand from Volodicheva's original shorthand dictation. For further details, see Yuriĭ A. Buranov, "K istorii leninskogo 'politicheskogo zaveshchaniya' (1922–1923 gg.)" ("On the History of Lenin's "Political Will" [1922–1923]"), *Voprosy istorii KPSS* (*Problems in the History of the CP CC*), no. 4, April 1991.]

It is the *only* handwritten original of the text dictated by Lenin on December 23, 1922, and it was written by an official of his secretariat. This handwritten document deviates from the typed version, which became the official text published in volume 45 of Lenin's *Polnoe sobranie sochinenii (Complete Works)*, which reads as follows:

Letter to the Congress.

I would strongly urge that at this Congress a number of changes be made in our political structure.

I want to tell you of the considerations to which I attach most importance.

At the head of the list I set an increase in the number of Central Committee members to a few dozen or even a hundred. It is my opinion that without this reform our Central Committee would be in great danger if the course of events is not quite favorable for us (and that [*i.e., a favorable course of events*—Ed.] is something we cannot count on).

Then, I intend to propose that the Congress should, on certain conditions, invest the decisions of the State Planning Commission[4] with legislative force, meeting, in this respect, the wishes of Comrade Trotsky—to a certain extent and on certain conditions.

As for the first point, i.e., increasing the number of CC members, I think this must be done in order to raise the prestige of the Central Committee, to do a thorough job of improving our administrative machinery, and to prevent conflicts between small sections of the CC from acquiring excessive importance for the future of the Party.

---

4. In Russian, the State Planning Commission is called Gosplan.

It seems to me that our Party has every right to demand
from the working class 50 to 100 CC members, and that
it could get them from it without unduly taxing the
resources of that class [*i.e., that it would not be difficult
to get them from the working class*—Ed.].

Such a reform would considerably increase the stability of our Party and ease its struggle in the encirclement
of hostile states, which, in my opinion, is likely to, and
surely will, become much more acute in the next few years.
I think that the stability of our Party would gain a thou-
sandfold by such a measure.

Lenin. 23.XII.22. Taken down by M.V.[5]

Let us examine the fourth paragraph of the official
published version. It reads:

Then I intend to propose that the Congress should on
certain conditions invest the decisions of the State Planning
Commission with legislative force, meeting, in this respect,
the wishes of Comrade Trotsky—*to a certain extent and
on certain conditions* [Italics added.]

The italicized words do not appear in the original handwritten text. This is the first variant reading that appears
in the typed version of the document, and it changes the
meaning considerably.

---

5. Lenin, *Polnoe sobranie sochinenii,* vol. 45, pp. 343-344; *Collected
Works,* vol. 36, pp. 593-594. The handwritten original, penned by N.S.
Alliluyeva, is reproduced in Appendix 2. The typewritten copy, typed
by M.A. Volodicheva, is found in RCPSMHD, f. 2, op. 1, d. 24047, and
is also reproduced in Appendix 2. [Editor's note: f = fond, meaning
"collection"; op = opis, meaning "list"; d = delo, meaning "file"; l = list,
meaning "page"; and sh = sheet.]

The change in meaning is even greater when the two readings of the next paragraph are compared. The typed version reads:

> As for the first point, i.e., increasing the number of the CC members, I think this must be done in order to raise the prestige of the Central Committee, to do a thorough job of improving our administrative machinery and to prevent conflicts between small sections of the CC from acquiring excessive importance for the *future* of the Party. [Italics added.]

In the original handwritten text, the last sentence reads:

> . . . from acquiring excessive importance for the "judges" of the Party.

The typed version looks quite unsuspicious, but the altered sentence, with the word *future* (without quotation marks), is edited in the style of the "will." The handwritten copy, where the word *"judges"* is used (it is no accident that this word is in quotation marks), is made in the style of a business document.

Who did Lenin call "judges"? The answer can be found in the "Letter to the Congress" dictated by Lenin on December 24, 1922, which begins:

> By stability of the Central Committee, of which I spoke above, I mean measures against a split, as far as such measures can at all be taken. For, of course, the whiteguard in *Russkaya Mysl*[6] (it seems to have been S.S. Oldenburg)

---

6. *Russian Thought*, a newspaper.

was right when, first, in the whiteguards' game against
Soviet Russia, he banked on a split in our Party; and when,
secondly, he banked on grave differences in our Party to
cause that split.[7]

In this text (closely related to the previous day's dictation
and similar in meaning and intention), Lenin names one of
the "judges" directly: S.S. Oldenburg, the émigré publicist
who expressed interests of political emigration. In one of
the variants (with the word *future*) the style of the article
is high-flown (let me say: Stalinist); in the other it is typically
the Leninist publicist style.

Further on we shall examine what caused the wording
in Lenin's text to change. Here let us regard the features
of another source. In the Russian Center for the Preservation
and Study of Modern History Documents (RCPSMHD, the
former Central Party Archives) a certain series of documents
were filed together in 1956, when Lenin's political will was
being prepared for publication. The cover card (which is
the original) reads:

Moscow. 7/Jul–1923.
        To Comrade Kamenev. Here is the material promised
by Comrade Kuíbyshev for the Party Archives.
                                        (The signature is illegible.)[8]

"The material promised," sent from the Central Control
Commission (CCC), consisted of several typescript copies

---

7. Lenin, *Polnoe sobranie sochinenií*, vol. 45, p. 344; *Collected Works*,
vol. 36, p. 594.

8. RCPSMHD, f. 17, op. 2, d. 790, sh. 1.

of Lenin's dictations from December 23–29, 1922. Originally this included a record from December 24–25, 1922 (the will). That this record was later withdrawn can be inferred from the short description of the documents attached to the file, which, for the record for December 23, 1922, reads:

> "Two suggestions to the Party Congress." 1. On increasing the number of CC members to 50 or 100 (as a measure for the stability of the CC). 2. On granting legislative functions to the State Planning Commission. (The idea was suggested by Trotsky.)

This contents sheet also reads:

> The second letter. 24/XII–1922. Development of the first suggestion on increasing the number of CC members (character descriptions).

Thus, soon after the Twelfth Congress, V.V. Kuíbyshev, having thoroughly studied Lenin's records, turned them over to the archives, which were under Lev Borisovich Kamenev's control. This occurred on May 18, 1924, a year before Lenin's wife, Nadezhda Krupskaya, turned the copies of Lenin's documents over to the CC, which up to that date, as their author wished and as all Party documents ensured, had been "carefully" kept in sealed envelopes in Lenin's secretariat and with his relatives.

With this in mind, let us examine the basis of the statement suggested at the beginning of this part. Historians generally share the view that Lenin decided not to offer his first record, dictated on December 23, 1922, to the Politburo and to the RCP(b)[9] CC members. I think what actually happened was different. Originally, Lenin planned a series of letters to the upcoming Twelfth Congress, as was his habit. But certain actions by Stalin and other Politburo members made him decide differently.

In fact, in the first installment of his "Letter to the Congress," dated December 23, 1922, Lenin writes in the style of an appeal to Politburo members or CC members: he uses such expressions as, "I want to tell you," "I intend to propose," and "It is my opinion." In other words, as Lenin had prepared a report for the Eleventh Congress, he again began, despite his extremely poor health, to prepare his report for the Twelfth.[10]

He assumed that there would be plenty of time before the launching of the Twelfth Congress and that the Politburo would be able to consider his suggestions. Also, he hoped that he would be able to recover and participate in the Congress.[11] It is worthwhile to note, too, that in another dictation he gave no orders that his notes were confidential. Volodicheva indicates in her December 23 entry in Lenin's journal:

---

9. RCP(b) = All-Russian Communist Party (Bolshevik).

10. On the eve of the Eleventh Congress of the RCP(b) Lenin was ill. On March 23, 1922, three days before the Congress began, he gave the plan of his report to the Congress in a letter to V.M. Molotov and asked him to approve it at the Plenum. He also asked, if possible, to allow him not to participate in the work of the Plenum. On March 27, Lenin delivered the political report of the CC. (See Lenin, *Polnoe sobranie sochinenii*, vol. 45, pp. 60–62; *Collected Works*, vol. 36, pp. 571–575.)

11. Lenin, *Polnoe sobranie sochinenii*, vol. 45, p. 477. As the journal testifies, Lenin asked his doctor on January 29, 1923 whether he could address the Congress on March 30. Answering in the negative, the doctor nevertheless promised that he "would be up and about" by that time.

A little after 9 Vladimir Ilyich called me to his flat. In the course of 4 minutes he dictated. Felt bad. Doctors were there. Before starting to dictate, he said: "I want to dictate a letter to the Congress. Take it down!" Dictated quickly, but his poor health was obvious. Toward the end he asked what the date was. Why was I so pale? Why wasn't I at the Congress? Was sorry that he was taking up the time that I could have spent there. I received no more orders.[12]

The next day, December 24, 1922, the situation suddenly changed. And it changed on Stalin's initiative. It is in the entry of the Records of Lenin's documents (September 1920 through January 1924), no. 8628, dated 23/XII: "To Stalin" ("V.I.'s Letter to the Congress").[13] This note shows that Stalin, the Party's General Secretary, received the text of the first part of "Letter to the Congress" the day it was dictated. Having read this, Stalin, who had the responsibility of ensuring the maintenance of the strict regimen that the doctors had prescribed for Lenin, called for a conference to be held the next day, December 24, at which he would be present along with Nikolaí Ivanovich Bukharin and Kamenev, who then decided to allow Lenin to dictate his "notes" on the condition that he "should not wait for an answer."[14] Any information about "political life" was prohibited.[15]

---

12. Ibid., p. 474.

13. RCPSMHD, f. 5, op. 4, d. 1, sh. 141.

14. Lenin, *Polnoe sobranie sochinenií*, vol. 45, p. 710.

15. On December 18, 1922, the resolution of the CC Plenum read: "Make Comrade Stalin personally responsible *for the isolation* of Vladimir Ilyich with regard to both his personal relations with officials and his correspondence." (*Izvestiya CPSU CC*, 1989, no. 12, p. 191.) [Italics added.] [Editor's note: *Izvestiya CPSU CC* (or, more exactly, *Izvestiya Tsk KPSS*) is an official Party magazine, not to be confused wtih the newspaper *Izvestiya*.]

Lenin, finding himself now in quite a different situation, decided to restrict all of his notes. Thus there appeared the characterizations of G.L. Pyatakov and the Politburo members, which went down in history as Lenin's will. The personal descriptions are of great importance, but there was another aspect to the matter: Lenin's analysis and estimation of the arrangement of the forces within the Politburo. From December 23–31, 1922, Lenin kept working diligently on his report for the CC at the Twelfth Congress. The confidential documents he dictated, which constituted in their entirety a "Letter to the Congress," he considered an integral part of the articles he was preparing for publication. These materials were meant to become the contents of his political report.

Stalin seemed to have understood this, and having full information about Lenin's health, moods, and behavior, he undertook a series of actions to strengthen his position in the Party. The overt conflicts between Stalin and Trotsky, beginning in December 1922, led Stalin to reword Lenin's document.

On December 21, 1922, Nadezhda Krupskaya, with the permission of one of Lenin's doctors, Professor O. Foerster, transcribed Lenin's letter and sent it to Trotsky, who at Lenin's request, adopted his position on the problems of the monopoly of foreign trade: "we should not stop and should continue the offensive" with the intention to prepare this policy for "the Party Congress." Having received the letter, Trotsky started carefully to fulfill Lenin's request.[16]

On December 22, Stalin began to hinder this undertaking, having received a letter from Kamenev written on or shortly before December 22:

---

16. *Izvestiya CPSU CC*, 1989, no. 12, p. 191.

Joseph,

Tonight Tr[otsky] phoned me, saying he had received a note from St[arik],[17] who, though he is happy with the congressional resolution on Vneshtorg,[18] wants Tr[otsky] to deliver a report on this question to a faction of the Congress and to prepare the ground to put this question to the Party Congress. Apparently, he means to strengthen his position. Trotsky did not offer his opinion, but he asked that this matter be handed over to the section of the CC responsible for the conduct of the Congress. I promised him to tell you about it, and I am doing this.

I could not reach you by phone.

In my report I am going to present the resolution of the CC Plenum with fervor. I shake your hand.

L. Kam[enev]

I will come tomorrow, as there is such a heap of materials for the report that I am drowning in it and can't manage it.

L.K.[19]

Stalin answered immediately:

22/XII.1922

Comrade Kamenev!

I have received your note. I think we should confine ourselves to the statement in your report without bringing this up at the faction. How did Starik manage to organize this correspondence with Trotsky? Foerster utterly forbade him to do it.

J. Stalin[20]

17. By "Starik" ("Old Man"), Kamenev means Lenin.
18. Vneshtorg = Ministry of Foreign Trade.
19. *Izvestiya CPSU CC*, 1989, no. 12, p. 191.
20. Ibid., p. 192.

The same day Stalin offended Krupskaya with "the rudest escapade," using "unbefitting swearing and threats." On this occasion Krupskaya wrote to Kamenev:

23/XII

Lev Borisych,

With regard to the short dictation I took from Vlad. Ilyich with his doctors' permission, Stalin dealt me yesterday with the rudest escapade. This is not my first day as a member of the Party—and during these 30 years I have not heard a single rude word from any of my comrades. The Party interests and those of Ilyich are no less dear to me than to Stalin. Now I need to exercise great self-control. I know better than any doctor what I may and what I may not tell Ilyich, as I know what agitates him and what does not. At any rate I know it better than Stalin. I am appealing to you and to Grigorií, as the closest friends of V.I., and I beg you to defend me from the rude interference into my personal life, from unbefitting swearing and threats. I don't doubt the unanimous decision of the Control Commission, with which Stalin took liberties to threaten me, but I have neither the strength nor the time to spend on this stupid squabble. I am a human being and my nerves are extremely strained.

N. Krupskaya[21]

As mentioned above, on December 23, 1922, Stalin learned from the document transcribed by Volodicheva (the first part of the "Letter to the Congress") that Lenin advised

21. Ibid., p. 192; Lenin, *Polnoe sobranie sochinenií, tom 54* (*Complete Works, vol. 54*), (Moscow: Izdatelstbo Politicheskoí Literatury, 1965), pp. 674–675.

that the State Planning Commission be reorganized, "meeting, in this respect, the wishes of Comrade Trotsky." On December 24 Trotsky sent Stalin a letter, proposing his own draft of the reorganization, not yet knowing that it had already been approved "on certain conditions" by Lenin. One must bear in mind that during the autumn of 1922 Lenin's position on the national question, which coincided with that of Trotsky, was completely opposite from Stalin's.

Analysis of the above documents leads to the conclusion that Stalin's position was strongly threatened. His personal interests pushed all else into the background, and he decided to alter Lenin's note of December 23, 1922. So it was not by accident that the "official" version of the record appeared in the series of documents received by Kuíbyshev, and later published in volume 45 of Lenin's *Complete Works*.

It is most likely that the text was "improved" sometime between December 24 and 29, 1922, when the CC members read Trotsky's letter describing his plans for the reorganization of the State Planning Commission and the CLD (the Council of Labor and Defense). Stalin joined Lenin's and Trotsky's discussion of the problem.[22] As mentioned above, Lenin's and Trotsky's positions on the problem came closer in December 1922.[23]

In January 1923 Stalin and Trotsky wrote each other on the issue of governing the country. Stalin wanted the Council of Labor and Defense to be at the head of the administrative machinery. Accordingly, the subordinates of the CLD chairman were now also to serve as the board of deputies for the chairman of the CPC (Council of People's

---

22. *Trotsky's Papers, 1917–1922*, vol. 2, Mounton, 1971, pp. 578–582.
23. Lenin, *Polnoe sobranie sochineniĭ*, vol. 45, pp. 349–353.

Commissars), increasing the number of deputies to five. In addition to this these five, the chairman of the State Planning Commission as well as the People's Commissariat for Finance were also to serve on this board. Stalin also suggested that Trotsky assume the post of one of the deputies of the CLD chairman and at the same time manage such a department as SEC (Supreme Economic Council).

According to Trotsky's draft, the task of unifying and directing the work of the state economy organs should be allotted to the State Planning Commission. The SEC was to become subordinate to the chairman of the State Planning Commission, and the SEC chairman was at the same time to be deputy chairman of the State Planning Commission. Assuming that his plan would be adopted, he apparently claimed the post of chairman of the State Planning Commission, and rejected the post offered him indirectly by Stalin.

Trotsky's idea about a special role for the State Planning Commission, which was supported by Lenin, and the personal rivalry between Stalin and Trotsky that Lenin foresaw, were involved in these mere administrative plans. On December 23, 1922, having agreed in general with Trotsky's proposed reorganization of the State Planning Commission, Lenin gave his specific opinion of the situation in a letter dated December 27, mentioning also that Trotsky should not be chairman of the State Planning Commission, as "personal matters are at present too closely interwoven with the question of principle."[24]

It was at about this time that Trotsky was given the text of Lenin's December 23 dictation, with the new wording.

---

24. Lenin, *Polnoe sobranie sochinenii,* vol. 45, p. 350; *Collected Works,* vol. 36, p. 599.

This coincided with another of Stalin's actions, the aim of which was not to divulge to Trotsky the information that Stalin received from Lenin's secretariat (as Trotsky, of course, expected that Lenin's first letter should have been followed by others). Stalin's action is quite explainable: Lenin's character descriptions of the two "outstanding leaders" of the RCP(b) CC favored Trotsky over Stalin.[25]

The literature concerning Lenin's political will confirms that, despite all the conspiratorial measures Lenin undertook to keep his notes secret, Stalin, and probably other Politburo members (Trotsky among them), read not only the record dated December 23, 1922, but also all the rest that he dictated over the next few days. Until now not a single document was known that would have led to the conclusion that Trotsky, like Stalin, was allowed full information. V.P. Naumov's interview, "Lenin's Will,"[26] only raised the question of whether Trotsky knew the contents of Lenin's will in the last ten days of 1922. Later "the obscurity" of Naumov's information was qualified by the Institute of Marxism-Leninism (which is attached to the CPSU CC): on February 26, 1988 *Pravda* "expressed the opinion that the Politburo and the RCP(b) CC members and some of the Party Central Committee members had been informed of some [of Lenin's] notes before May 18, 1924 [when Krupskaya delivered the will to the RCP(b) CC], at least those dictated before December 29, 1922." Naturally, after this publication, readers' letters were sent to the CPSU CC asking who had read the

---

25. Lenin, *Polnoe sobranie sochinenii*, vol. 45, p. 345; *Collected Works*, vol. 36, pp. 594–596.

26. "Leninskoe zaveshchanie" ("Lenin's Will"), an interview with V.P. Naumov, *Pravda*, February 26 and March 25, 1988.

will in December 1922. Naumov's interview suggested that the will was known to Trotsky. In 1990 *Izvestiya CPSU CC* published two letters (Fotieva to Kamenev and Kamenev to Stalin dated 29/XII-1922). The foreword stated that, "This question is to some extent answered with the published letters of Kamenev and Fotieva."[27] This careful wording by experienced archivists of the Central Party archives of the Institute of Marxism-Leninism, which published the letters, is not accidental. The crux of the matter is that these newly published documents do not solve the mystery of whether Trotsky had read Lenin's will. An analysis of the documents suggests the following sequence of events:

In the late evening of December 29, 1922, Lenin's secretary, Lidia Aleksandrovna Fotieva, unexpectedly came to her direct chief, Kamenev (who was the deputy chairman of the Council of People's Commissars under Lenin, and currently held the duties of acting chairman), and "first verbally and then in writing" made her declaration. Kamenev immediately sent the text of her declaration to Stalin.

Fotieva wrote:

> 29/XII–22.
> On Saturday, 23/XII, Comrade Stalin was given the letter Vladimir Ilyich wrote to the Congress, which had been taken down by Volodicheva. Meanwhile, after the letter had already been given [to him], it was found out that Vladimir Ilyich wished that this letter be kept in strict confidence in the archives, that it could be opened only by himself or by Nadezhda Konstantinovna, and could be shown to others only after his death. Vladimir Ilyich is

---

27. *Izvestiya CPSU CC*, 1990, no. 1, p. 157.

quite sure that he said this to Volodicheva while dictating the letter. Today, 29/XII, Vladimir Ilyich called for me and asked whether such instructions had been made on the letter, and he said again that the letter should be made public only after his death. Taking into account Vladimir Ilyich's weak health, I found it impossible to tell him that *a mistake was made*, and I assured him that the letter was not known to anybody and that his instructions were carried out.

I ask those comrades who have come to be acquainted with the letter that, in case they speak to Vladimir Ilyich in the near future, under no circumstances are they to tell about the mistake or to give him any occasion to believe that the letter is known; and I ask them to consider this letter as the record of the opinion of Vladimir Ilyich, which should not have been known by anybody. [Italics added.]

29/XII–22. L. Fotieva.[28]

In his turn, Kamenev added the following note to Fotieva's declaration, and directed this to Stalin:

To Stalin

Comrade L.A. Fotieva came to me today, 29/XII, at 23 o'clock and first verbally and then in writing made the above declaration. I think it is necessary to let this be known to those CC members who know the contents of Vladimir Ilyich's letter. (I know that its contents are known to Comrades Trotsky, Bukharin, Ordzhonikidze, and you.) I neither told nor hinted to anybody about this letter. I think neither did any of the above listed comrades. But if some of them revealed the contents of the letter to other

---

28. Ibid., pp. 157–158.

CC members, they should be informed of Comrade Fotieva's declaration.

L. Kamenev[29]

What follows from Fotieva's declaration? As we see, she writes that sometime between December 23 and 29, 1922, only the record of the beginning of "Letter to the Congress," dated December 23, was sent to Stalin from Lenin's secretariat. From Kamenev's postscript to Fotieva's "declaration," it appears, in turn, that the contents of this document alone were known to Kamenev, Trotsky, Bukharin, Ordzhonikidze, and Stalin. So Fotieva, Kamenev, and Stalin left for history a document with the statement that it was only the record dated December 23 that was sent to the CC from Lenin's secretariat by "mistake." But what was Volodicheva's mistake, if on December 23 she wrote in Lenin's journal that Lenin did not give any orders about the confidentiality of his letter?

As Volodicheva testified, she received such an order only on December 24, 1922. We shall return to this evidence, but for now let us note that other sources also indicated that the Politburo and CC members were acquainted with Lenin's will (dated December 24). As mentioned above, Kuíbyshev and Kamenev knew its contents by May 1923, and there is other direct evidence. In August 1923 Bukharin and Zinovyev were corresponding with Stalin. We shall explore this correspondence in detail later, but for now let us mention that, although Bukharin and Zinovyev knew the contents of Lenin's will, Stalin wrote frankly that he knew nothing about it.[30] Thus those who knew the contents of the December

---

29. Ibid., pp. 158–159.

30. *Izvestiya CPSU CC*, 1991, no. 4, p. 205.

23 note were Stalin, Bukharin, Trotsky (who received the revised text), Kuíbyshev, Ordzhonikidze, and Kamenev. The circle of those who, as the sources irrefutably testify, knew the text of the records dated of December 24–25, 1922 was much narrower: Bukharin, Zinovyev, Kuíbyshev, and Kamenev.

In December 1922 Kuíbyshev was Secretary of the CC. Could the CC secretary avoid informing the General Secretary, his immediate superior, about the document he had received? Of course not. But, as before, approval was not given to turn Lenin's document over from Lenin's secretariat to Stalin between December 24 and 29, 1922.

At the same time, Lenin's journal testifies that he warned Volodicheva twice about the confidentiality of the notes: the first time was on December 24; the second time, as Fotieva declared in writing, was on December 29. In Kuíbyshev's (and, thus, in Stalin's) possession were found only the documents dated December 29. Stalin used these documents to lead Trotsky to think that it was impossible to get additional information about Lenin's further dictations. To prevent Trotsky from comparing the altered letter with the original, Stalin (passing aside those who knew the original contents of the text, such as Krupskaya), sent him a copy of Fotieva's declaration, writing on it: "I have read. Stalin. To Comrade Trotsky only." In turn, Trotsky also left his inscription: "I have read. It goes without saying that I told none of the CC members about Vladimir Ilyich's letter. L. Trotsky."[31] As far as we know, Trotsky never mentioned this episode again. Most likely, he never understood that Stalin had deluded him.

---

31. *Izvestiya CPSU CC*, 1990, no. 1, p. 157.

On June 2, 1923 Krupskaya turned over the notes that Lenin had dictated toward the end of 1922 to Zinovyev. (I will discuss this in detail later.) Afterwards, it was decided to send them to members of the Politburo. On June 8, 1923 Trotsky informed the CC Secretariat that he had not yet received these documents.[32] So Trotsky did not read these dictations, and in particular he did not know that they contained Lenin's thoughts on the State Planning Commission (dictated on December 27), which was of great interest to him.

Thus, the documents published by the Institute of Marxism-Leninism (attached to the CPSU CC) and their interpretation by researchers did not answer the question as to whether Trotsky had read Lenin's will in December 1922. But in April 1992 some new documents surfaced. I am of the opinion that the information contained in them, if compared with earlier documents, settles the matter. In December 1922 Stalin, having read Lenin's will, concealed it from Trotsky. At the same time he distorted the text of Lenin's first note, thereby falsifying it.

---

32. Yuriĭ Felshtinskiĭ, ed., *Arkhiv Trotskogo. Kommunisticheskaya oppozitsiya v SSSR, 1923-1927* (*Trotsky's Archives: Communist Opposition in the USSR, 1923-1927*) (Moscow: Terra, 1990), vol. 1, p. 56.

Two

Running the Blockade

On January 23, 1923, Lenin made an attempt to run the political blockade organized by the General Secretary. In but a single line of his article, "How We Should Reorganize the Workers' and Peasants' Inspection,"[1] he made it known to everybody that he did not approve of the extreme strengthening of Stalin's power. The manuscript of this article was delivered to *Pravda*'s editorial office by Lenin's sister, Mariya Ilyinichna Ulyanova, on January 23.

Upon receiving information about the article, Stalin's first maneuver was to prevent its publication. The first step, however, was taken by Bukharin, editor of *Pravda*. Later, at the Thirteenth Party Congress, E.A. Preobrazhenskii described this matter in this way:

---

1. In Russian, the Workers' and Peasants' Inspection is called Rabkrin, short for <u>Ra</u>boche-<u>kr</u>estyanskaya <u>In</u>spektsiya.

Comrades, I was sitting in *Pravda*'s editorial office when Comrade Lenin's article had already been set in type. It was delivered to *Pravda* and was immediately typeset, as nobody doubted that Comrade Lenin's article could not be postponed. When Mariya Ilyinichna came to the office, she spoke of the necessity of publishing Comrade Lenin's article the next day. Comrade Bukharin, having read the article, said, "I can't allow this article to be published." He phoned Comrade Stalin, read some excerpts from the article, and said that the article should not be published. After that the Politburo was called and the matter was discussed there.[2]

This passage from Preobrazhenskii's speech was missing in the shorthand report of the conference, and it was not published. In July 1923 Stalin removed Preobrazhenskii from *Pravda*'s editorial staff. Further historical accounts of the delay in publishing the article were described variously by those who participated in the decision. In a letter to the Party CC, dated October 23, 1923, Trotsky unambiguously asserted that at first he alone, but later with Kamenev's support, was in favor of the publication of Lenin's article, but that the Politburo was against it. Trotsky also said that Kuibyshev suggested that only one copy of *Pravda* containing the article on the Workers' and Peasants' Inspection be printed, especially for Lenin. In their response to Trotsky's letter, all the members of the Politburo denied this allegation. In 1924 the opponents of publication, the same Politburo members, affirmed that there had been no delay and that the matter had been discussed with only one purpose in

---

2. RCPSMHD, f. 51, op. 1, d. 4, sh. 110.

mind: to explain to the Party that Lenin's article did not attest to a possible split in the CC, but that it was merely a result of his worsening condition.

Let us emphasize that the published version of Lenin's article had been edited. Most likely Trotsky was not a party to this editing. The complete text of the article, without Stalin's alteration, was published as early as 1956. The comparison of the two paragraphs from the texts of Lenin's article, published in *Pravda* on January 25, 1924 and in the journal *Communist* in 1956, makes a vivid psychological impression and testifies to the high level of the "editors" (probably Bukharin) or professional politicians and journalists from the General Secretary's apparatus. One can only guess Lenin's emotions when he read his article, in which but one phrase was missing.

The complete text of the eighteenth paragraph of Lenin's article reads:

Our Central Committee has grown into a strictly centralized and highly authoritative group, but the conditions under which this group is working are not commensurate with its authority. The reform I recommended should help to remove this defect; and the members of the Central Control Commission, whose duty it will be to attend all meetings of the Politburo in a definite number, will have to form a compact group which should not allow anybody's authority without exception, *neither that of the General Secretary, nor of any other member of the Central Committee,* to prevent them from putting questions, verifying documents, and, in general, from keeping themselves fully informed of all things and from exercising the strictest control over the proper conduct of affairs. [Italics added.][3]

The words italicized above were omitted. The same day, January 25, 1923, Bukharin, the editor of *Pravda*, and two members of the CC Secretariat (Kuíbyshev and Molotov) were asked to edit all the materials that were published in the Party newsletter, *K podgotovke partiínogo syezda* (*The Preparation of the Party Congress*).

In 1924, during the next stage of the inner-Party struggle, the question of publishing Lenin's article was brought up again, this time on the initiative of Sapronov, who supported Trotsky. In his speech at the Second Khamovniki[4] District Conference in January 1924, Sapronov repeated Trotsky's accusation that Stalin did not want to publish Lenin's article. Meanwhile, as early as the autumn of 1923, Trotsky addressed the CC in a letter, which, in part, read:

But what was the attitude of the Politburo to the draft of the "Reorganization of the Workers' and Peasants' Inspection" proposed by Comrade Lenin? Comrade Bukharin did not dare publish Comrade Lenin's article, who, for his part, insisted on its immediate publication. N.K. Krupskaya told me about this article over the telephone and asked me to intervene so that the article could be published as soon as possible. At a meeting of the Politburo immediately called at my suggestion, all those who were present— Comrades Stalin, Molotov, Kuíbyshev, Rykov, Kalinin, and Bukharin—were not only opposed to Comrade Lenin's draft,

---

3. Lenin, *Polnoe sobranie sochinenií*, vol. 45, p. 387; *Collected Works, Volume 33* (Moscow: Progress Publishers, 1966), pp. 481–486.

4. A district within the city of Moscow.

but were also opposed to the publication of the article itself. The members of the secretariat opposed this sharply and utterly. Comrade Lenin had insisted that the article be shown to him in print. Comrade Kuíbyshev, the would-be People's Commissar of the Workers' and Peasants' Inspection, suggested at this Politburo meeting that a special copy of *Pravda* be printed with the article by Comrade Lenin in it to calm him down, but at the same time to conceal the article from the Party. I proved that the crucial reform proposed by Comrade Lenin was progressive in itself—of course, on the condition of its proper realization—but even if one has a negative attitude to this suggestion, it would be ridiculous and absurd to protect the Party against Comrade Lenin's suggestions. I was answered with formalistic arguments: "We, the CC, we are responsible; we decide." I was supported on this matter only by Comrade Kamenev, who was nearly an hour late to the Politburo meeting. The chief argument in favor of publishing the letter was that Lenin's article could not be concealed from the Party.[5]

Nevertheless, in 1924, at the Khamovniki conference, Kamenev, who, of course, remembered everything, answered Sapronov in the following way: "You have said," declared Kamenev addressing Sapronov, "that most Politburo members were opposed to publishing Lenin's article. What does that mean politically? It means that the Politburo was going to conceal Lenin's opinion from the Party. If this is so, where are your guarantees that we are not concealing anything today or that we shall not conceal anything tomorrow?"[6]

---

5. *Izvestiya CPSU CC*, 1989, no. 11, p. 181.
6. Ibid., p. 183.

The reaction of the audience to these words was sudden. As the shorthand report testifies, voices were heard: "Perhaps you will." Kamenev continued confidently: "If there are any comrades who think that the Politburo consists of persons who were going to conceal Lenin's opinions and who can conceal opinions tomorrow, then such Politburo [members] should be removed this very day." The conference ordered an inquiry to ascertain "whether the facts in Comrade Sapronov's concluding remarks and those of other speakers were correct."[7] Thus, on January 10, 1924 a special commission of the Khamovniki Conference asked Sapronov about the problem. In reply, he repeated what had already been told to him by Trotsky and Preobrazhenskií.

At the same time it was ascertained by a meeting of the commission that Sapronov, being a CC member, knew about the events in general because "of talks with other CC members." But Sapronov did not know that Lenin's article had been reworded.

Not satisfied with the information received from Sapronov, the commission found it necessary to hear from the immediate participants in the events, i.e., "all Politburo members, and Kuíbyshev, Bukharin, and Preobrazhenskií, as well," and other "persons named by Comrade Sapronov." On February 11, 1924 the commission's "query" was sent to the Politburo members of the RCP CC as well as to CC members Preobrazhenskií and Pyatakov. It contained a request to answer the following questions:

---

7. Ibid., p. 184.

(1) Is it true that the Politburo did not want to publish Ilyich's article and was going to print a special copy of *Pravda* for Ilyich?
(2) If so, the commission requests a detailed explanation as to why this question arose, and whether it took place at the Politburo meeting or in a private conversation.
(3) If not, we ask for a reason as to why Comrade Sapronov made his declaration at the Khamovniki District Conference.[8]

On February 23, 1924 Kuíbyshev answered these questions. He affirmed that there was not a single vote against publishing the article, but that the suggestion to delay publishing was discussed. The Politburo's decision was "to publish it immediately and to inform local organizations by a special letter, supported by all the Politburo members, saying that the Politburo was unanimous in all crucial questions."[9] As for his own participation in the solution to the problem, Kuíbyshev said that he had been in favor of publishing the article, though he had had only a consultative vote (as he was not a Politburo member). At the same time Kuíbyshev affirmed that before the Politburo meeting, at which a "nervous atmosphere" prevailed, he expressed "aloud" his "brief thoughts" in the following manner: "If Ilyich is ill, and if this illness is reflected in the article, and if it is necessary to show Ilyich a published copy, perhaps a special copy of *Pravda* should be printed?"[10] Thus, as it was quite impossible to deny the undeniable, Kuíbyshev reduced the

8. Ibid., pp. 187–188.
9. Ibid., p. 188.
10. Ibid., p. 189.

importance of the whole matter, maintaining that the Politburo did not discuss the article, and that all doubts and suggestions were of an unofficial character, as they had taken place before the Politburo meeting.

Stalin answered the commission's question on March 4, 1924, much later than Kuíbyshev. After apologizing for his delay, he repeated Kuíbyshev's answers, but in a more precise manner, and explained the reasons why Sapronov had made his declaration in a very strong manner.

Stalin wrote, ". . . the reason is that a factional squabble had emerged from the condition of the bitter inner-Party struggle." He called Trotsky's October 23, 1922 declaration, which blamed Kuíbyshev for his attempt "to shelve Comrade Lenin's article on the Workers' and Peasants' Inspection," to be "an indubitable slander."[11]

Let us sum up some conclusions which we may infer from this exposition. Stalin, with the assistance of his supporters, took the opportunity of Lenin's illness in December 1922 to attempt to squeeze him out of the country's political life. By this action a situation was deliberately created in which Lenin was forced to make secret his political report for the upcoming Party Congress. Being fully informed of Lenin's work, the General Secretary also excluded Trotsky, whom he had reason to consider his number one rival in the struggle for Party leadership. At the same time Stalin began to alter Lenin's dictations. The latter is proved by the survival of Alliluyeva's original copy of Lenin's text of December 23, 1922, and by the abridging of Lenin's article on the Workers' and Peasants' Inspection, published in *Pravda* in January 1923. Trotsky did not know about the

---

11. Ibid., p. 192.

original wordings of Lenin's texts. The evidence of Stalin's intrusion into Lenin's texts was found many years later: the original wording of the article on the "Workers' and Peasants' Inspection" was only discovered as the text of Lenin's *Complete Works* was being prepared for publication in 1956; but the records dated December 23, 1922, were not discovered until 1989. Since the other handwritten reports of Lenin's dictations of December 1922 were burned, it is impossible to prove whether Stalin reworded any of the other texts and documents that became known as Lenin's will. But the above-mentioned "editorial" intrusions by the General Secretary into Lenin's documents leave open the great probability of equally or more serious falsifications of everything Lenin dictated from December 1922 through early January 1923. This statement is based on the following fact. Trotsky was the only person then who did not fear declaring that falsifications had occurred. However, Stalin managed not only to cut him off from all information coming from Lenin, but also skillfully to deceive him. It is possible that Stalin could make Trotsky believe that Lenin's suggestions, in his article on the "Workers' and Peasants' Inspection," concerning the reform of the Party machinery, were untimely. In any case, although Trotsky supported the publication of Lenin's article, he at the same time wrote (for himself) the following letter, dated January 27, 1923:

Top Secret
LETTER TO LOCAL COMMITTEES
AND REGIONAL COMMITTEES

Dear Comrades,
   Pravda no. 16 from January 25 published Comrade

Lenin's article, "How We Should Reorganize the Workers' and Peasants' Inspection." One paragraph of this article talks about the role of our Party CC and the undertaking of organizational measures that would either prevent or greatly hamper the possibility of a split in the CC, if the relationships between the proletariat and peasantry became aggravated due to novel conditions resulting from NEP.[12]

Some comrades pointed out to the Politburo that the comrades in the provinces could misinterpret Comrade Lenin's article to mean that the inner life of the CC has recently found a bias *to the split*, and that the CC made Comrade Lenin put forward some organizational suggestions in his article. In order to eliminate the very possibility of such conclusions, which are far removed from the reality of the situation, the Politburo and Orgburo consider it necessary to let the Local Committees know the circumstances that made Comrade Lenin write his article.

Comrade Lenin's return to his extremely hard work after his illness resulted in overstrain. The doctors considered it necessary to prescribe that Comrade Lenin do absolutely nothing for a certain period, and forbade him even from reading newspapers (because reading newspapers is, for Comrade Lenin, of course, neither entertainment nor rest, but, like all his usual political tasks, it provokes hard mental work). It goes without saying that Comrade Lenin does not take part in the Politburo meetings and that the minutes of the Politburo and Orgburo meetings are not even sent to him (also in strict accordance with what the doctors had prescribed). But the doctors considered it permissible to allow Comrade Lenin, as full mental leisure is unbearable for him, *to keep a kind of*

---

12. NEP = New Economic Policy.

a *diary*,[13] where he writes down his thoughts on various problems, and some parts of this diary, by order of Comrade Lenin himself, appear in the press. The environment in which the work on the article was carried out shows that the proposals in this article were influenced not by some complications within the CC, but by Comrade Lenin's general considerations of the difficulties that lay ahead for the Party in the future historical epoch.

Not going into the discussion of the possible historical dangers (the question raised by Comrade Lenin in his article) in this mere informational letter, the Politburo and Orgburo members, in order to avoid possible misunderstanding, consider it necessary to declare quite unanimously that in the CC inner workings *there are no circumstances at all that would give any reasons to fear "a split."*

This explanation is given not to the press, but in a top secret letter, in order not to give enemies an opportunity to bring troubles and embarrassment by false information about Comrade Lenin's health. The CC does not doubt that if the alarming conclusions, mentioned at the beginning of the letter, were drawn from Comrade Lenin's article in the provinces, the Local Committees will immediately give the proper orientation to the Party organizations.

The members of the Politburo and Orgburo of the RCP CC: Andreev, Bukharin, Dzerzhinskii, Kalinin, Kamenev, Kuíbyshev, Molotov, Rykov, Stalin, Tomskii, Trotsky

Moscow 27
January 1923

(M. Burakova)[14]

---

13. Editor's note—"Diary" here apparently means "dictations." This is not to be confused with the diary of events maintained by Lenin's secretaries.

14. Ibid., pp. 179–180.

Trotsky received from the doctors considerable information about Lenin's health. Most likely in January 1923 he had already decided that Lenin's death was imminent and that was why he placed all his hopes only in himself. This was what most likely would determine his behavior, when Lenin undertook a last attempt to run the political blockade organized by the General Secretary.

Three

The Last Attempt

From December 30 to 31, 1922, Lenin dictated a text on the national question, which later came to be known as "The Question of Nationalities or 'Autonomization'." This was another response to the General Secretary in the prolonged discussion of the methods of creating the USSR. The events preceding this dictation were as follows. On September 15, 1922 the CC of the Communist Party of Georgia, having discussed Stalin's theses on the establishment of the USSR on autonomous grounds, supported the entry of Georgia into the Soviet Union, "while preserving all the attributes of independence." Stalin, having informed Lenin about this in his letter dated September 22, appreciated this position as the opinion of "independent socialists." But Lenin did not agree with the General Secretary. The October 1922 Plenum of the Party CC failed to resolve the question the way Stalin would have preferred, and tension was not reduced. Being on Stalin's side, Ordzhonikidze tried to bring the opponents of "autonomization" to reason in a rather unusual way. He called one

45

of the opponents "a fool and a provoker," and as a last resort slapped him in the face. On October 19, 1922, the CC of the Communist Party of Georgia decided to ask Moscow to be admitted into the Union, not as part of a Transcaucasian federation, but separately as a Transcaucasian republic. The secretary of the Communist Party CC of Georgia, M. Okudzhava, was then immediately dismissed by a decision of the Transcaucasian Territorial Committee.

The VKP(b) CC commission, with Dzerzhinskii at the head, was sent to Georgia, and approved "the position" of Ordzhonikidze, who was a direct supporter of Stalin. Upon his return on December 12, Dzerzhinskii told Lenin everything that had happened. The Party leader's illness did not permit him to react immediately, but the thought remained that Stalin had made a blunder in this situation. Thus, in the text dictated from December 30–31, 1922, Lenin overtly accused the chief initiator of the "Georgian incident" of administrative arbitrariness. He called him "a real and true 'national-socialist'," and even a vulgar "Great Russian bully." This character description (in addition to Lenin's evaluation of Stalin expressed on December 24–25, 1922)[1] without doubt concerned Ordzhonikidze and Dzerzhinskii. Lenin wrote: "I also fear that Comrade Dzerzhinskii, who went to the Caucasus to investigate the 'crime' of those 'nationalist-socialists,' distinguished himself there by his truly Russian frame of mind (it is common knowledge that people of other nationalities who have become Russified overdo this Russian frame of mind) and that the impartiality of his whole commission was typified well enough by Ordzhonikidze's 'manhandling'."[2]

---

1. See Appendix 2.
2. Lenin, *Polnoe sobranie sochinenii*, vol. 45, p. 358; *Collected Works*, vol. 36, p. 606.

In the end, having sharply condemned all participants of "the incident," Lenin singled out its chief initiator. "I think," he wrote, "that Stalin's haste and infatuation with pure administration, together with his spite against the notorious 'nationalist-socialism,' played a fatal role here. In politics, spite generally plays the basest of roles."[3]

It is worthwhile to note that on January 24, 1923, not having found in *Pravda* his article on the "Workers' and Peasants' Inspection," Lenin asked Fotieva to question Dzerzhinskii or Stalin about the commission's materials in the Georgian case. At the same time he asked his secretariat to investigate all the materials about the question. "The purpose is," the journal of Lenin's secretaries reads, "to report to Vladimir Ilyich, who wanted this for the Party Congress." This diary entry is another indication that Lenin was systematically working on his speech for the Party Congress.[4]

A further chronicle of these events indicates that Lenin was still interested in the problem, and that he was waiting for the materials in order to complete the section about national politics, but that Stalin tried to prevent him from doing that. On January 25, 1922 Lenin asked Fotieva whether the materials had been received from Dzerzhinskii. On January 27, having still not received them, Fotieva sent Stalin a letter. On January 29 Stalin answered that he could not release the materials without the Politburo's decision. On the same day Fotieva reported that, having learned about this, Lenin "said that he would fight to get the materials."[5]

---

3. Lenin, *Polnoe sobranie sochinenii*, vol. 45, p. 357; *Collected Works*, vol. 36.

4. Lenin, *Polnoe sobranie sochinenii*, vol. 45, p. 476.

5. Ibid., p. 477.

In fact, he was fighting already for all the parts of his report at the same time, a section of which must have been concerned with the principles of the establishment of the USSR, principles that differed from those espoused by Stalin. Thus, on January 26, having switched to developing the principles of the Party's reorganization, Lenin asked his secretary to give "instructions for Tsyurupa, Sviderskií, and Avanesov to be told that if they agree with his article [on the Workers' and Peasants' Inspection], they should arrange a number of conferences and discuss by way of preparation for the Congress."

On February 1 Lenin again requested the materials for the Georgian case. Upon learning that the materials had been received, he asked for their quick treatment. On February 14 Lenin explained to Fotieva that, besides other matters, this issue "agitated him most of all," and he asked "to hurry things up" in preparing the Georgian question.

Fotieva was also given the following orders: "a hint be given to Soltz" [A.A. Soltz, member of the presidium of the Central Control Commission, RCP(b)] that Lenin "was on the side of the injured party. Make some of the injured understand that he was on their side. Three points: (1) One should not fight. (2) Concessions should be made. (3) One cannot compare a large state with a small one. Did Stalin know? Why didn't he react? The name 'deviationist' for a deviation toward chauvinism and Menshevism proves this very deviation of the great-power chauvinists."[6]

On March 3 Lenin received Fotieva's memo about the collected materials with the appendix. It read that the

---

6. Lenin, *Polnoe sobranie sochinenií*, vol. 45, p. 607; "Gruzinskií intsident" ("The Georgian Incident"), *Pravda*, August 12, 1989.

declaration by A. Kabakhidze (whom Ordzhonikidze had slapped in the face) "was lost." It was substituted with A.I. Rykov's letter, who was present at the clash in Ordzhonikidze's apartment in Tiflis. (Rykov wrote that the clash was of a personal character.) A series of documents was added that described the mood in the CC on this problem and recorded Fotieva's and Zinovyev's conversation. There were many in the CC whose attitudes toward the situation were as follows:

> Sergo [Ordzhonikidze] became an inveterate liar, but Stalin supported him instead of stopping him. It is 20 percent Sergo's fault.
> . . . If it were not for the authority of the CC, then Makharadze would have the majority in the Party [in the CP of Georgia CC]. A compromise (of the three with Stalin) is taking shape. Two respected comrades, Kuíbyshev and Bukharin or Kamenev, are being sent to their Congress [of the CP of Georgia]. The opponents of Ordzhonikidze's position are Zinovyev, Bukharin, Kamenev (hesitant). The compromise is to make some of the deviationists come back. [As for] Zinovyev [and] Ordzhonikidze: they must remain. [As for] Stalin: he can be sent to Turkestan for a year.[7]

Having gotten acquainted with the materials, Lenin asked Volodicheva to dictate a letter to Trotsky:

> Top Secret.
> Personal.
>
> Dear Comrade Trotsky!
> It is my earnest request that you undertake the defense

---

7. Ibid.

of the Georgian case in the Party CC. This case is now under "persecution" by Stalin and Dzerzhinskií, and I cannot rely on their impartiality. Quite the contrary. I would feel at ease if you agreed to undertake its defense. If you should refuse to do so for any reason, return the whole case to me. I shall consider it a sign that you do not accept.

With best comradely greetings.
Lenin.[8]

To this letter was added the following note:

Comrade Trotsky: To the letter communicated to you by phone, Vladimir Ilyich asked to add for your information that Comrade Kamenev is going to Georgia on Wednesday [March 7], and [Vladimir Ilyich] wants to know whether you wish to send anything there yourself.[9]

For the second time, as at the end of December 1922, Lenin sought Trotsky's help. Trotsky answered quickly. That same day, according to M.A. Volodicheva, Trotsky declared that since he "is ill, he cannot undertake the defense. But as he hopes to be well soon, he asks us to send him the materials (if nobody needed them) so that he could get acquainted with them. If his health permitted, he would read them." He also added that "he does not even know if he will be able to address the Congress; that he is quite paralyzed; that he had to write the theses on industry and has strong doubts that his health would permit him to do this; that at

---

8. Lenin, *Polnoe sobranie sochinenií*, vol. 54, p. 329; *Collected Works*, Volume 45 (Moscow: Progress Publishers, 1970), p. 607.

9. Ibid.

present he is interested in the question raised by Vladimir Ilyich on the reorganization of the Workers' and Peasants' Inspection; and that, if it is possible, he would like to have a talk with him on this question, if he is allowed to work as much." Besides, Trotsky informed Lenin that "he spoke to Makharadze, to Mdivani, heard Ordzhonikidze, and declared at the CC Plenum that, though he hesitated, he is now assured that blunders had been made."[10] The latter was quite true. Notes exchanged between Lenin's secretary Glyasser and Trotsky, written at the February Party CC Plenum, reflect Trotsky's position on the Georgian case. Glyasser wrote:

> Comrade Trotsky!
> You said at the discussion on the national question that you had had doubts during the adoption of the decision on the Georgian conflict, but now (during the discussion) you confirmed that this decision was mistaken and that Ordzhonikidze's position at the Caucasus was wrong. Did I understand you correctly?

Trotsky answered:

> I don't quite understand why you are asking this question. Are you recording the minutes of the discussion? I said approximately this: if I had some doubts of the rightness of the politics of Ordzhonikidze and the Politburo, these doubts are now a hundredfold stronger after Ordzhonikidze's speech.[11]

---

10. RCPSMHD, f. 5, op. 2, d. 34, sh. 3; *Izvestiya CPSU CC*, 1990, no. 9, p. 149.

11. RCPSMHD, f. 5, op. 2, d. 34, sh. 2-2 obverse; *Izvestiya CPSU CC*, 1990, no. 9, p. 153.

This note is interesting in many respects. Of course, Trotsky understood that Glyasser was defining his position more precisely in order to inform Lenin. Having put Glyasser in her place and having hinted that she exceeded her commission, as her task was simply to take shorthand, Trotsky gave the necessary explanation of his position.

In early March, Trotsky was ill, having caught a cold while hunting. At the same time he was very busy preparing the theses for his report to the upcoming Congress. But was he so busy as to refuse to comply with Lenin's request?

We have an opportunity to follow the rhythm of Trotsky's work, in order to see to what extent he was busy in March 1923. The archive file contains a series of papers on which he was working day after day. These papers indicate that he worked very hard, even though he was ill. At the same time he had time for very prosaic things. For example, on March 2 he worked on a letter to the People's Commissar for Finance, Sokolnikov. (At Sokolnikov's suggestion, this was related to the change of the contents of Trotsky's theses.) That same day he composed a paper on the question of army financing.

On March 3, Trotsky sent the photographer Otsup the following note:

Why did you send me these silly photos? We agreed that you would do one photo for Comrade Anenkov. And Comrade Anenkov promised to destroy the photo and you promised to destroy the negative. The photo is of absolute buffoonery. It must not be reproduced under any circumstances.

This note has a later message written on it:

The negatives have been destroyed. See the commission act from March 4.[12]

To write this correspondence on the destruction of the negatives and to glance through documents pertaining to some acts, Otsup's explanations, and so forth, took Trotsky several days! At the same time, on March 5, he informed the Politburo:

> About a week ago the doctors promised me that I would feel better a week later. But two days ago I felt worse again because of working two hours at my desk. I don't know what is going to happen. . . .[13]

That same day he wrote:

> Top Secret. To all Politburo members. To Comrades Smilga, Pyatakov, and Bogdanov.
> I sent a handwritten copy of the first part of my thesis on industry, which I have corrected based on the discussion and amendments I have received. I am going to send the second part tomorrow. The wording is not final, as I have had to correct by dictating, and without a pen in my hand.[14]

In short, being very busy with his report and his photos, Trotsky said that he could not find the time for the problem of special importance raised by Lenin. Thus, Trotsky did not support Lenin, and apparently he did not wish to have an overt fight with Stalin and with a group of his adherents

---

12. RCPSMHD, f. 325, op. 1, d. 412, sh. 5.
13. Ibid., sh. 22.
14. Ibid., sh. 26.

in the Politburo. Nevertheless, being alone, Lenin continued fighting. The documents reflect the course of his struggle in the following way.

On March 5, 1923 Lenin received much negative information. This was dangerous for him, partially paralyzed, suffering the defects of brain blood circulation disorder. Having been refused by Trotsky, Lenin learned from his wife, probably that same day, details of her clash with Stalin. Lenin received the information about the General Secretary's rudeness to Krupskaya in two stages. First, in the last ten days of December 1922, Krupskaya, omitting the details, told her husband about this. Mariya Ilyinichna Ulyanova, Lenin's sister, recollects in her memoirs:

> The doctors insisted that V.I. be told nothing about business. One should have been very careful, especially with N.K., whose habit was to share everything with V.I. Sometimes she would do it quite involuntarily, and she would blab out against her wishes. The Politburo charged Stalin with seeing to it that the doctors' orders not be violated. But one day, having apparently learned about a conversation between N.K. and V.I., Stalin phoned her and began to explain to her rather sharply, apparently believing that V.I. would not learn about this conversation, that she should not talk business with V.I., otherwise he would call her before the Central Control Commission. N.K. was extremely agitated about the conversation. She was beside herself, sobbed, and even rolled on the floor, and so forth. *Several days later* she told V.I. about the reprimand, adding that she and Stalin had already made up. In fact, Stalin had phoned her and apparently attempted to soften the unpleasant impression made on N.K. with his reprimand and threat. But she told Kamenev and Zinovyev about

Stalin shrieking to her on the phone, and apparently mentioned the Caucasian affairs. [Italics added.][15]

Krupskaya's letter to Lev Kamenev, dated December 23, 1922, and reprinted above on page 24, complained about Stalin's rudeness. As a result of these events, Stalin apologized to Krupskaya, apparently following Kamenev's advice. But Krupskaya, as Mariya Ulyanova testifies, did not tell Lenin at first the whole truth. She did not tell him that she had informed Kamenev and Zinovyev about the conflict. But what she told him was enough for Lenin to write quite sharply about Stalin's rudeness in his character descriptions. Perhaps this information, though incomplete, was enough to embellish Stalin's characterization. For in his dictation of January 4, 1923, Lenin wrote:

Stalin is too rude, and this defect, although quite tolerable in our midst and in dealings among us Communists, becomes intolerable in a General Secretary.[16]

In March 1923, Stalin was again anxious about a possible rapprochement between Lenin and Trotsky. Taking into account the bad experience he had had in December 1922, when he attempted to make a frontal assault upon the relationship between Lenin and Trotsky, he endeavored now to act more skillfully. Ulyanova describes Stalin's actions as follows:

---

15. *Izvestiya CPSU CC,* 1989, no. 12, p. 198.

16. Lenin, *Polnoe sobranie sochinenii,* vol. 45, p. 346; *Collected Works,* vol. 36, p. 596.

One morning Stalin called me to V.I.'s study. He looked very upset and distressed. "I could not sleep all night," he said to me. "What does Ilyich take me for? His attitude toward me! As if I were a traitor. I love him with all my heart. Tell him this, anyhow." I felt sorry for Stalin. He seemed to grieve quite sincerely.

Ilyich called me in for some reason or other, and I told him, incidentally, that his comrades sent him their best regards. "Ah, and what about Stalin?" he asked. "Stalin asked me to give you his best regards, too, and asked to say that he loves you so." Ilyich sneered and said nothing. "Well," I asked, "shall I give him your best regards, too?" "Do, please," Ilyich replied rather coolly. "But Volodya," I went on, "Stalin is a clever man, isn't he?" "He's not at all clever," Ilyich retorted decisively, and he winced.[17]

Further on, Ulyanova indicated that Lenin received further information concerning the conflict between Stalin and Krupskaya:

I did not say anything more; but *a few days later* V.I. learned that Stalin had spoken rudely with N.K., *and that both K[amenev] and Z[inovyev] knew about it. So in the morning, looking very upset,* he asked me to bring a stenographer to his room, asking first whether or not N.K. had left for the People's Commissariat for Public Education, and I said that she had.[18]

---

17. *Izvestiya CPSU CC*, 1989, no. 12, pp. 198–199.

18. Lenin, *Polnoe sobranie sochinenií*, vol. 54, pp. 329–330; *Izvestiya CPSU CC*, ibid., p. 199.

Having learned that some Politburo members were involved in the incident, Lenin could no longer regard this as merely a personal clash. Apparently he considered that not only was his personal honor at stake, but also his authority as the Politburo and Party leader. Thus, having called for Volodicheva, Lenin dictated the following letter to Stalin:

Top Secret. Personal. Dear C[omrade] Stalin!

You have been so rude as to summon my wife to the telephone and use bad language. Although she has told you that she was prepared to forget this, the fact nevertheless became known through her to Zinovyev and Kamenev. I have no intention of forgetting so easily what has been done against me; and it goes without saying that what has been done against my wife I consider to have been done against me as well. I ask you, therefore, to think over whether you are prepared to withdraw what you have said and to make your apologies, or whether you prefer that relations between us should be broken off.

Respectfully yours, Lenin.

5/III–23.

This letter was sent at once, but was delivered to Stalin on March 7, 1923. In turn, the General Secretary answered with the following note:

Strictly personal.

Comrade Lenin,

About five weeks ago I had a talk with Comrade N. Konstantinovna, whom I consider to be not only your wife, but also my old Party comrade, and I told her (over the telephone) approximately the following: "The doctors have forbidden us to give political information to Ilyich, and they consider this regimen to be the best medicine to cure him. But you, Nadezhda Konstantinovna, seem to have broken this regimen; one should not play tricks with Ilyich's life," etc.

I do not believe that one could see anything rude or impermissible undertaken "against" you, as I had no purpose other than your recovering as soon as possible. Moreover, I thought it my duty to look after the regimen. My explanation to N. Kon. proves that it was a silly misunderstanding.

However, if you consider it in order that I "withdraw" the above said words in order to preserve our "relations," I can withdraw them, but I fail to understand what the matter is, what my "fault" is, and, in fact, what you want from me.

J. Stalin[19]

Lenin could not read this letter yet, for his health had deteriorated, and on March 10 he suffered a severe stroke that disabled him completely. The journal of Lenin's doctors attests to his grave condition (March 10, 1923):

In the morning Vladimir Ilyich spoke with difficulty, often trying to find the right words. We [the doctors] came to Vladimir Ilyich at 1:15. Vladimir Ilyich spoke rather badly, could not find many words, and his articulation was not good. Because of recurrent spasms and continuous speech

---

19. RCPSMHD, f. 2, op. 1, d. 26004, sh. 3; *Izvestiya CPSU CC*, 1989, no. 12, p. 193.

defects, and according to the decision reached together with Foerster, we administered an intravenous injection. But the injection did not prevent further spasms. Approximately a quarter of an hour later there occurred a spasm again, this time more serious and more prolonged, which resulted in complete aphasia and paresis of the right facial nerve. His consciousness is quite clear. Vladimir Ilyich understands questions and either nods or shakes his head in response. Sometime later he could say "yes" and "no." The spasm started at two o'clock. The doctors spent the whole day in the apartment and by turn, every quarter of an hour, went into the Vladimir Ilyich's room with Vasilii Vasilyevich. The paresis of the facial nerve remains the same. He speaks separate words. They seem to be not always what he wants to say. He cannot say any coherent, except it be short, phrase.[20]

Meanwhile, Stalin strove to conclude the Georgian incident, adopting the line he needed with the assistance of Kamenev. On March 7, 1923, Kamenev informed Zinovyev:

Top sec[ret]
7.III.1923, 4 o'clock

Dear Grigorii,

I am leaving in two hours. I wish to inform you about the following facts in order for you to consider the situation. Having learned that the Georgian Congress is planned for March 12, Starik got very excited, nervous, and (1) he sent a written request for Trotsky "to undertake the defense of the G[eorgian] case in the Party, which will put me

---

20. RCPSMHD, f. 16, op. 2, d. 13, sh. 98–180; *Kentavr*, 1991, October–December, pp. 111–112.

at ease." Trotsky did not reply definitely. He called me last night for a consultation. (2) He wrote a letter of two lines, agreeing in practice with Mdivani and company, thus disavowing Sergo, St[alin], and Dz[erzhinskiĭ]. This he gave me to hand deliver to "Mdivani, Makh[aradze], etc.," (with a copy for Trotsky and Kamenev).[21] (3) He sent a personal letter to Stalin (with a copy for me and for you), which you must have already received. Stalin answered with a very reserved and sour apology, which can hardly be satisfactory for Starik.

I shall do all my best to reach peace at the Caucasus on the basis of the decisions, which could *unite* both groups.

I believe it will be possible to obtain this. But I fear that this will not satisfy Starik, who apparently wants not only peace in the Caucasus, but also definite *organizational conclusions at the top.*

I think you should remain in Moscow all the time and keep in touch with me in Tiflis. The Congress is postponed until April 15, which enables us to discuss all the conclusions derived from the facts once again. I am sorry that I have no time to talk to you before my departure.

I shake your hand.

L. Kamenev[22]

In turn, the General Secretary also informed Ordzhonikidze about the temporary compromise in the struggle against "the deviationists":

---

21. This letter can be found in Appendix 2.
22. *Izvestiya CPSU CC*, 1990, no. 9, p. 151.

Moscow

Dear Sergo!

I have learned from Comrade Kamenev that Ilyich is sending a short letter to Comrade Makharadze and others aligning himself with the deviationists and lashing out at you, Comrade Dzerzhinskií, and myself. Obviously there is a desire to turn the will of the Congress of the Communist Party of Georgia in favor of the deviationists. It goes without saying that the deviationists, on receiving this short letter, will use it to its utmost against the Transcaucasian Regional Committee, especially against you and Comrade Myasnikov. This is my advice:

1. The Transcaucasian Regional Committee should exert no pressure on the will of the majority of the Communist Party of Georgia in order to permit this will, at last, to show itself in full, whatever it is.

2. To achieve a compromise, but one that can be reached without any undue pressure on the majority of the responsible officials of Georgia, i.e., a natural voluntary compromise.

3. I was told that Comrade Myasnikov would like to come to the Congress, but he is said not to be permitted due to the want of laborers. I think he ought to be permitted as a delegate of the Party Congress, as I do not doubt that he will be chosen to the Party Congress.

Yours, J. Stalin

7.III.23. Moscow

P.S. The Congress has been postponed until the 15th [of April]. The Plenum is set for the 10th of April. Come in time.

J.St.[23]

---

23. *Izvestiya CPSU CC*, 1990, no. 9, pp. 151–152.

In the end, Stalin led his line: On March 26, 1923, Mdivani, the leader of the deviationists, was removed "to another post" by a decision of the Politburo, and Trotsky avoided an overt struggle and could not pass his suggestion about the recall of Ordzhonikidze from Georgia. But the chief blow was still awaiting Trotsky.

Four

Creating a Precedent

On April 16, 1923, the eve of the launching of the Twelfth RCP(b) Congress, Stalin fulfilled one of his complicated political intrigues: he made up his mind not to allow the publication of one of Lenin's most important articles, his letter on the national question. The General Secretary thus repeated the trick he had already tried at the end of December 1922. We remember that Stalin, with Fotieva's assistance, had cut Trotsky off from any information from Lenin's secretariat. Now he endeavored to place Lenin's article on a secret list and at the same time to compromise Trotsky.

At 5:35 p.m. Kamenev received the following memo from Fotieva after having had a telephone conversation with her:

Copy

COMRADE KAMENEV.
A COPY FOR COMRADE TROTSKY

Lev Borisovich,

In addition to our telephone conversation, I wish to inform you, as the Politburo chairman, of the following:

As I have already said to you on 31/XII-22, Vladimir Ilyich dictated his article on the national question.

He was much concerned with the question and he was making preparations to speak about it at the Party Congress.

Shortly before his last illness, he told me that he would publish this article, but sometime later. After that, he fell ill without having given a definitive order.

V.I. considered his article to be a directive and he attached great importance to it. In accordance with the order of Vladimir Ilyich, Comrade Trotsky was informed about it; V.I. charged him to defend his views at the Party Congress due to their solidarity on the question.

The only copy of the article I possess is kept, by V.I.'s order, in his secret archives.

I am informing you about what has been said above.

I could not do it earlier, as I have begun working only today after being ill.

Comrade Lenin's Personal Secretary.
L. Fotieva

16 April 1923[1]

Upon receiving this memo, Kamenev sent the documents to the CC. In his covering letter he wrote that Fotieva's memo

---

1. RCPSMHD, f. 325, op. 1, d. 412, sh. 149; *Izvestiya CPSU CC*, 1990, no. 9, p. 156.

meant nothing to him, but that "the CC should at once resolve the question of publishing Lenin's article in the affirmative." At the same time he answered Fotieva by letter, noting some discrepancies in her information. For example, he noted that Trotsky had shown him Lenin's article; and that Trotsky, referring to Fotieva, had drawn his attention "to its full and absolute secrecy," saying that it "should not be publicized in the press or even in orally." This discussion between Trotsky and Kamenev had taken place sometime after March 10, 1923, when Lenin could not give any other instructions. So Kamenev wrote to Fotieva reasonably about the "disagreement" between what she had told Trotsky and what she had written to him.

Kamenev's behavior was adroit. Having emphasized his objectivity (as he was in favor of publishing the article), he helped Fotieva (and, in fact, Stalin, who supported her) get out of the strange situation in which she found herself—strange because, in her letter to Kamenev, she affirmed simultaneously that (1) Lenin was going to publish the article, but he did not give a definitive order to do so; (2) he gave the article over to Trotsky, "due to their solidarity on the question." Kamenev seems not to have been satisfied with this latter statement, and he asked Fotieva in his note, "If you are sure that you know Vladimir Ilyich's wishes in this matter, you should make your definite suggestion to the CC at once."[2]

As we shall see, Kamenev helped Fotieva find the "definite suggestion" regarding Lenin's wishes. At the same time, Kamenev seems to have tired of the role given him by Stalin. As for Fotieva's appealing to Kamenev rather than Lenin on

---

2. RCPSMHD, f. 323, op. 1, d. 35, sh. 1–2; *Izvestiya CPSU CC*, 1990, no. 9, p. 157.

December 29, 1922, she did so to formally observe the procedural rules, as Kamenev was Lenin's second in command in the Council of People's Commissars. Now he had a reason to write to Fotieva, "As there is no post of 'chairman' in the Politburo (a [different] chairman is chosen at every meeting), I am surprised that you have appealed to me instead of following the usual Party procedure: going through the CC Secretariat."[3] Thus, with Fotieva's assistance, Kamenev let the General Secretary know that he should look into this matter himself, and that he could count, as usual, on his support.

Trotsky's reply—sent to "all RCP(b) CC members"—to Comrade Fotieva's letter included copies of Lenin's three notes from March 3, 1923. He explained that he had been working on the text of an article, received from Lenin, as "he took it as a basis for his emendations of Stalin's theses on the national question." The General Secretary took Lenin's remarks into account and, having been corrected, they were published in *Pravda* on March 24, 1923.

Trotsky suggested that the CC members be informed about the contents of Lenin's article and continue working in accordance to them. For his part, Trotsky promised not to raise the question of the article independently, as it "contains sharp accusations about three members of the CC. . . . If none of the CC members, for inner-Party reasons, raises the question of informing the Party or the Party Congress about the articles, then I shall consider this to be a silent decision that cancels my personal responsibility for this article, at least as far as the Party Congress is concerned."[4]

---

3. Ibid.

4. RCPSMHD, f. 325, op. 1, d. 412, sh. 147; *Izvestiya CPSU CC,* 1990, no. 9, p. 158.

Trotsky's desire to compromise with Stalin and his adherents, and his attempt to avoid a personal clash with the General Secretary concerning the article's publication, are here expressed clearly enough. But Stalin, unlike Trotsky, decided to take an aggressive stance. Not only did he put his rival in the Party leadership in an awkward position; he also achieved, by using the method developed by Lenin for solving controversial questions, his main goal of preventing the article from being published. Lenin oftentimes, in cases such as this, would limit consideration of the matter to those within the CC, or, at least to those at the Party Congress, thus withholding such information from most Party members at large. In short, Stalin based his actions on Lenin's procedural methods for dealing with especially important problems, preventing rank-and-file Party members from learning of the most crucial problems, especially those concerning the top leaders.

On April 16, 1923, at nine o'clock, the General Secretary received the following letter from Fotieva, who seems to have been working closely with him.

Comrade Stalin,

I have today discussed with Mariya Ilyinichna whether Vladimir Ilyich's article, which I sent you, should be published, since he indicated that he was going to publish it in connection with his proposed speech at the Congress.

Mariya Ilyinichna said that if there was no direct order from V.I. to publish this article, it should not be published; though she thinks members of the Congress should be informed about it.

Personally, I think it necessary to add that V.I. did not consider this article to be complete or ready for publication.

16/IV–23
9 o'clock p.m.

L. Fotieva[5]

Stalin was glad that a reason to prevent publication of Lenin's article was now available. It is worthwhile to note that in subsequent years the General Secretary defended himself from the accusation that he had prevented publication of the article, by claiming that the decision not to publish came from Lenin's own family.

Later the same evening, Stalin dealt Trotsky a serious blow by sending the following document to RCP(b) CC members.

Comrade Stalin's Declaration to CC Members

I am very surprised that Comrade Trotsky, though he received, as late as March 5th of this year, Lenin's articles—which are, of course, of principal importance—found it possible to hold them for more than a month without informing the Politburo of the CC Plenum about it until the eve of the Twelfth Party Congress. It is said, according to Congress delegates, that rumors and legends have arisen among the delegates about these articles—rumors and legends that are known, I have learned today, by people who have nothing to do with the CC; and that CC members themselves have to depend on these rumors and legends. It is clear that the CC should have been informed about their contents first.

I think that Comrade Lenin's articles should be pub-

---

5. RCPSMHD, f. 5, op. 2, d. 34, sh. 18; *Izvestiya CPSU CC*, 1990, no. 9, p. 159.

lished. One should regret that they have not been. However, it has become clear from Comrade Fotieva's letter that Comrade Lenin has not permitted them to be published, since he has not yet reviewed them.

10 o'clock p.m.

16/IV–23

J. Stalin[6]

The battle concerning Lenin's paper on the national question was now transferred to the Twelfth Party Congress, during which the fate of the article was decided by the two leaders. Lenin had foreseen their duel for power in the Party, but ultimately could not prevent the conflict. On April 17, 1923 Trotsky spoke with Stalin about his "declaration." The next day the General Secretary received Trotsky's request to disavow his attack.

Personal, no copies

COMRADE STALIN,

Yesterday, after our personal conversation, you said that you considered it quite clear that I did not make any wrong decisions about Comrade Lenin's article, and that you would prepare a written declaration to that effect.

I have not received this declaration as of 11 o'clock this morning. Perhaps yesterday's report prevented you from writing it.

In any case, you have not disavowed your first declaration, and this allows some comrades to spread a mistaken version among themselves.

For reasons you can easily understand, I cannot allow the slightest misunderstanding in this matter. I consider

---

6. RCPSMHD, f. 5, op. 2, d. 34, sh. 19.

it necessary to clarify the situation as soon as possible. If, in response to this note, I do not receive word from you to the effect that you will send the declaration to all the members of the Central Committee, which would exclude all possibility of any ambiguity on this question, I will consider that you have changed your mind, and I shall apply to the conflict commission for a full consideration of the case.

You, better than anybody else, can appreciate that the reason I have not yet done so is not that it would damage my interests.

18/IV-23[7]

In the end, Stalin avoided a public confrontation with Trotsky, and succeeded in preventing the publication of Lenin's article through the Presidium of the Twelfth Party Congress, which adopted the following resolutions:

Excerpt from Minutes No. 2
of a meeting of the Presidium of the
Twelfth RCP(b) Congress
18 April 1923

Agenda:

1. Comrade Lenin's notes on the national question, in particular on the Georgian question.

Resolution:

---

7. RCPSMHD, f. 325, op. 1, d. 412, sh. 152; *Izvestiya CPSU CC,* 1990, no. 9, p. 161.

1.a) To publicize Comrade Lenin's notes as well as all relevant material at the meeting of the Council of Elders;

b) After which Presidium members should publicize these materials again among Congress delegations.

c) At the same time, the resolutions of the CC Plenum on the Georgian question should be conveyed to the Council of Elders.

d) The note mentioned above and the materials on the national question are not meant for publication by the press.

Agenda:

2. The question of informing RCP CC members about the contents of Comrade Lenin's note on the national question on the eve of the Twelfth RCP Congress, i.e. on 16/IV.

Resolution:

2. The Presidium of the Twelfth RCP Congress confirms that Comrade Lenin's note on the national question became known to the CC on the eve of the Congress quite independently of the will of any CC member and only in connection with Comrade Lenin's orders during the course of his illness.

In this connection the Presidium considers it a calumny to spread any rumors about attributing the delay in this note's publication to any CC member.[8]

---

8. *Izvestiya CPSU CC*, 1990, no. 9, p. 162.

The last paragraph of the second resolution, as we can see, withdrew any inference of Trotsky's guilt in the delay of publishing Lenin's note. Nonetheless, among CC members, suspicions remained that Trotsky had played a special part in withholding Lenin's article. And in this sense Stalin's plan was realized, though not fully.

However, the chief result of Stalin's intrigues was quite different. At the Twelfth Party Congress a precedent was created: Lenin's document was taken into consideration only by the privileged Party elite, and information about it was denied to rank-and-file members. Moreover, the Party elite did not discuss Lenin's suggestions.

Five

Repeat

The recently published diaries of Lenin's doctors provide an interesting picture. After his stroke in March 1923 and until his death Lenin was incapable of controlling political events.[1] From March 1923 to May 1924 there was an acute struggle for power within the Party. In his struggle with Trotsky, Stalin gathered all the rest of the members of the Politburo around him, and he attached great importance to concealing Lenin's last documents.

Stalin aimed not only to isolate Lenin's materials from rank-and-file Party members, but, as far as possible, to restrict them to the highest echelons of power. However, Stalin was aware that Lenin's behavior was unpredictable.[2]

---

1. "Dnevnik dezhurnogo vracha V.I. Lenina v 1922-1923 gg." ("The Diary of Lenin's Doctor on Duty, 1922-1923"), *Kentavr*, March–April 1992, pp. 106-121.

2. An example of Lenin's unpredictability was his unexpected journey to Moscow from his residence in Gorki on October 19, 1923.

Only Lenin's death in January 1924 allowed Stalin to accomplish his goal with some assurance of success.

Meanwhile, in spite of Lenin's illness, Krupskaya made a number of attempts to circulate Lenin's documents. This kept Stalin under constant pressure. She sought to protect Trotsky as far back as the autumn of 1923, soon after the October Plenum of the Party's Central Committee at which he suffered a defeat. In a letter to Zinovyev dated October 31, 1923, Krupskaya wrote:

> ... in this disgraceful affair ... Trotsky is not the only one to blame; our group also is guilty: you, Stalin, and Kamenev. If you couldn't do this, that would prove the total powerlessness of our group, as well as its absolute helplessness. No, it is not that we cannot do it; we do not want to do it. We assumed an incorrect and inadmissible stance. We cannot allow an atmosphere in which we squabble and settle private scores.
>
> The workers ... would strongly blame not only Trotsky but all of us. The sound instinct of the working class would speak strongly against both parties, but especially against our group as being responsible for the general tone.
>
> That's why everyone fears that this squabble will leak to the masses. It is necessary to conceal the incident from the workers. But leaders who shall hide something from workers ... might not venture to say everything to them. What is this? It should not be this way.
>
> ... It is good that I was absent when Petrovskií made the charge that Trotsky is responsible for Lenin's illness. I would have cried; the charge is false. Lenin was worried not about Trotsky but about the national problem and the morals of our seniors. You know that Vladimir Ilyich saw

the danger of a split not only because of Trotsky's private characteristics, but also those of Stalin and others. And therefore, as you know, the references to Lenin were inadmissible and insincere. It is impossible to allow them. They were hypocritical. For me, these references are an intolerable torture. I thought: what is the point of his recovering when his most intimate colleagues have such an attitude toward him, and hardly consider his point of view, and distort it.

. . . The moment is too serious to foster a split and to make Trotsky's work psychologically impossible. . . . At present, Trotsky has had to bear the entire odium for disunity. He has been blamed, but in reality wasn't Trotsky driven to it?[3]

In June 1923, as if testing again the patience of Stalin and his associates, she began to deliver Lenin's documents to the Party's leadership. As a result, Trotsky learned early that month that, in December 1922 (after prolonged discussions between themselves), Lenin had in fact actually taken his side regarding the State Planning Commission problem. The notes about the State Planning Commission that Lenin dictated on December 27-29, 1922, were only published in the USSR after the Twentieth Party Congress, together with Lenin's other documents of late 1922.[4]

It is interesting to note that the collection of documents edited by Yuriĭ Felshtinskiĭ in 1990 contains the "Summary of Comments by Members of the Politburo and the Presidium of the Central Inspection Commission Concerning Comrade

---

3. *Izvestiya CPSU CC*, 1989, no. 2, pp. 201-202.

4. Lenin, *Polnoe sobranie sochineniĭ*, vol. 45, pp. 349-353; *Collected Works*, vol. 36, pp. 598-611.

Zinovyev's Proposal on the Publication of 'Lenin's Will'."[5]
There is a mystery that only the editor can unravel: who
first used the phrase "on the Publication of 'Lenin's Will',"
and when? The point is that in June 1923 the Politburo and
Presidium of Central Committee members discussed, not the
"Letter to the Congress," but the notes about the State
Planning Commission that Lenin dictated on December 27–
29, 1922, which later became known as "Granting Legislative
Functions to the State Planning Commission."

Krupskaya delivered these notes to Zinovyev after she
delivered Lenin's articles "On Cooperation" and "On Our
Revolution" to the Central Committee for their disposal.[6] It
is important to note that Krupskaya delivered the note "On
the State Planning Commission Problem," as Zinovyev called
it, separately from the articles "On Cooperation" and "On
Our Revolution."

On June 2, 1923, after receiving the notes on the State
Planning Commission, Zinovyev sent the following note to
Stalin:

Copy.
Proposal of Comrade Zinovyev.
To the Politburo of the RCP CC.
To Comrade Stalin.
N.K. Ulyanova-Krupskaya handed me Vladimir
Ilyich's notes on the State Planning Commission problem.
Owing to the great importance of these notes, I suggest

---

5. Yuriĭ Felshtinskiĭ, ed., *Arkhiv Trotskogo. Kommunisticheskaya
oppozitsiya v SSSR, 1923–1927* (*Trotsky's Archives: Communist Opposition in the USSR, 1923–1927*) (Moscow: Terra, 1990), vol. 1, p. 56.

6. Both these articles were published in *Pravda*: "On Cooperation,"
May 26–27, 1923; "On Our Revolution," May 30, 1923.

that we make them available to all members and candidate members of the Central Committee of the Russian Communist Party, as well as to members of the Presidium of the Central Inspection Commission. I enclose a copy of the said notes.

G. Zinovyev

2.VI.23[7]

"The said notes" on the State Planning Commission problem were first read, not by all members and candidate members of the Central Committee, but only by members of the Politburo; by Bukharin, a Politburo candidate member; by members of the secretariat of the Central Committee; and by Soltz, the representative of the Presidium of the Central Inspection Commission. At a discussion on whether or not to publish the notes, Zinovyev, Kamenev, and Stalin argued against doing so, saying in particular that the article contained personal character descriptions (the names of Krzhizhanovskii, Pyatakov, and Trotsky were actually mentioned in the text). Besides, Kamenev considered these notes to be a "non-delivered speech at the Politburo"; in other words, he maintained that they were not intended for the press (which at that time went without saying).

Following are brief comments that reflect the position of the majority of the Central Committee members concerning the question of only one of the fragments of Lenin's report to the Twelfth Congress.

---

7. RCPSMHD, f. 17, op. 2, d. 790, sh. 12.

Top Secret.

Copy.

SUMMARY
OF COMMENTS OF POLITBURO AND PRESIDIUM OF
CENTRAL INSPECTION COMMISSION MEMBERS
ON COMRADE ZINOVYEV'S PROPOSAL

1. "I think it is necessary to publish this article if there are no formal reasons that would prevent this. Is there any difference in the methods of the distribution of this article and others (on cooperation, about Sukhanov)?"

   Trotsky

2. "It is impossible to publish; it is a non-delivered speech at the Politburo. Nothing else. It is based on personal characterizations, and such is its [only] content."

   Kamenev

3. "Nadezhda Konstantinovna also was of the opinion that it should be distributed only to the Central Committee. I didn't ask about publication, because I thought (and think) that it is excepted. One can raise this question. There was no difference in the distribution, except that this note (about the State Planning Commission) was handed over to me later, several days ago."

   Zinovyev

4. "I think that there is no necessity to publish; the more so, that the sanction for publication from Ilyich is absent."

   Stalin

5. "I am in favor of Zinovyev's proposal: to acquaint only the members of the Central Committee; not to publish, because the general public will not understand."

   Tomskií

6. "This note of Vladimir Ilyich was not meant for the general public, but for the Central Committee, and therefore he paid great attention to the description of persons. The paper on cooperation has nothing like that. It should not be published."

A. Soltz

7. Comrades Bukharin, Rudzutak, Molotov, Kuíbyshev— in favor of Zinovyev's proposal.[8]

Thus, Trotsky was the only person who argued in favor of publishing "On the State Planning Commission Problem." Now aware of Lenin's position on reorganizing the State Planning Commission, Trotsky, who had once promised to remain silent, was no longer, after Lenin's death, bound by this promise. However, having taken into account the will of the majority, he could not have his own way. As a result, Lenin's document was hidden from the Party. All persons mentioned in the "Summary of Comments," except for Trotsky, were on Stalin's side: Zinovyev, Kamenev (these two, together with Stalin, were already famous as the "troika"), as well as Bukharin, Kuíbyshev, Soltz, and Tomskii.

One of the many problems arising from Lenin's death was the publication of the notes that he dictated from the winter of 1922/23, through the spring of 1923. The government communiqué concerning his death stated that there were no visible signs of his imminent demise; it was noted that his "death came suddenly and unexpectedly." The appeal, "To the Party, To All Workers," said: "Lenin lives in the hatred of Leninism, Bolshevism, and Communism, in the

---

8. Ibid., sh. 13.

camp of our enemies," and "the Party will go forward by an iron step," because "it has in its hands that will that Comrade Lenin left for it."[9] The ambiguity in the claim about the hatred of Lenin could not hide the cynicism concerning his will. All his later articles and dictations were still deliberately hidden, not only from the Party, but also from those who were close to him.

Stalin's active resistance against any attempt to publish Lenin's notes was carried out in two stages. In the first stage, from 1923 through 1924, he developed and approved a rationale to explain the causes for hiding Lenin's last works from the Party. During the second stage, from 1925 through 1927, owing to an aggravated inner-Party struggle, this rationale was subjected to a serious test—for, during the struggle for leadership, Kamenev and Zinovyev, Stalin's co-authors and direct participants of his plan, became his opponents and insisted on publishing the will. Stalin's resolve not to publish Lenin's last works withstood this test.

The scheme Stalin followed was simple: he claimed that since Lenin did not give clear instructions to publish his notes, only the highest body of the Party, its Congress, could decide their fate. In this case, Stalin referred to the testimony of Lenin's sister, Mariya Ilyinichna Ulyanova, emphasizing that he himself had always supported the publication of Lenin's works. Stalin had maintained this position since the spring of 1923.

The first test of this position, as noted above, was the Twelfth Party Congress; the second test followed at the Thirteenth Congress. On May 18, 1924, five days before the

9. *Proletarskaya revolutsiya* (*The Proletarian Revolution*), 1924, no. 3, pp. 7–8.

beginning of this Congress, Krupskaya stated that she had delivered 13 notes that Lenin had dictated between December 24, 1922 and January 16, 1923. A portion of Krupskaya's statement was published in volume 45 of Lenin's *Complete Works*. The complete text of her statement follows.

I delivered notes that Vladimir Ilyich dictated during his illness from December 23 to January 23: 13 separate notes. The note on the national problem is not among these (it is in the hands of Mariya Ilyinichna). Some of these notes have already been published ("On the Workers' and Peasants' Inspection," "On Sukhanov"). The unpublished notes are from December 24–25, 1922 and January 4, 1923, which include the personal descriptions of some of the Central Committee members. Vladimir Ilyich expressed a strong desire that, after his death, these notes should be brought to the attention of the Party Congress.

18.V.24.

N. Krupskaya[10]

Kamenev wrote a note underneath Krupskaya's text:

I received the documents that Comrade N.K. Krupskaya requested be delivered to the Commission of the Plenum of the Central Committee. 18 May 24.

L. Kamenev[11]

A further postscript read:

---

10. RCPSMHD, f. 17, op. 2, d. 790, sh. 15–16.
11. Ibid., sh. 16.

The above listed notes by Vladimir Ilyich, handed over to Comrade Kamenev, constitute the documents with which I am well acquainted, and which V.I. intended to bring to the Party's notice.

N. Krupskaya

18.V.24

End of the record.

L. Kamenev
N. Krupskaya[12]

This small sheet of paper ended with the following decision, signed by six persons:

Having become acquainted with the documents handed to Comrade Kamenev on 18.V.24 by Krupskaya, the Commission of the Plenum of the Central Committee decided to bring them to the attention of the nearest Plenum of the Central Committee with the proposal to bring them to the attention of the Party Congress.

19.V.24

G. Zinovyev	N. Bukharin
A. Smirnov	J. Stalin
M. Kalinin	L. Kamenev[13]

Krupskaya's insistence on the necessity of informing the Party Congress about Lenin's last thoughts was clearly evident in her controversial attitude toward the publication of the corresponding notes made by Lenin's secretaries. She assumed that the Congress would determine the fate of the documents, and hoped that it would support their publi-

---

12. Ibid., sh. 16–16 obverse.
13. Ibid., sh. 16 obverse.

cation. Her speech at the July 1926 Plenum of the Central Committee confirms this. Krupskaya emphasized that Lenin wrote his notes for the Party, but that he did not find the time to give accurate instructions regarding their presentation to the Party. The Thirteenth Congress, as Krupskaya noted, decided the fate of the documents, though they had been intended for all the Party.[14]

In reality, the Plenum of the Central Committee, convened on May 21, 1924, had predetermined the fate of Lenin's notes. A decision was made at this Plenum based on Kamenev's report, which said that according to Lenin's wishes, the reading of the documents should be postponed until the Congress, that they should be read to the delegations, and that it should be established that these documents are not subject to reproduction, and are to be read to the delegations by the members of the Commission of Ilyich's papers.

Since the verbatim record of the Plenum is inaccessible to investigators, it is impossible to accurately reconstruct the agenda on this question. This verbatim record was never made, or it was destroyed, or it has not yet been found in the recesses of the former Party's archives. Thus, investigation must be limited to the memories of the participants of these events.

On August 9, 1923, the former secretary of the Orgburo, Boris Bazhanov, was appointed assistant of Stalin's Central Committee. As he claims, all the most important decisions at the Politburo had been previously coordinated by the "troika"—Kamenev, Zinovyev, and Stalin. (In addition to Bazhanov and two other assistants named Mekhlis and Kanner, Stalin had yet another assistant, I.P. Tovstukha,

---

14. RCPSMHD, f. 17, op. 2, d. 246(IV), sh. 64.

who specifically dealt with the organization of the Lenin Institute.)

Although competent historians consider sources such as Bazhanov's memoirs of great importance, they also maintain a certain amount of skepticism. It is clear that after Bazhanov's emigration from the USSR he could not use many materials. Further, memory not only keeps or buries the past; it also transforms it in various ways. Nevertheless, I shall cite below an extract of Bazhanov's memoirs that describes the situation at the Plenum on May 21, 1924, when Lenin's will was read aloud for the first time. It is important to refer to this extract for at least two reasons: first, his memoirs have always been rejected with disdain by Soviet historiography; and, second, the attempts by official Party historians of the Institute of Marxism-Leninism (attached to the CPSU CC) to detail the circumstances in which Stalin was able to cut the Party off from the will, have failed.

In March 1964 a special conference was held at the Institute of Marxism-Leninism to which the surviving delegates of the Thirteenth Party Congress were invited.[15] These delegates were asked to relate what they remembered about Lenin's will and about its presentation at the Congress.[16] An examination of the verbatim record illustrates that the surviving participants of that Congress either remembered very little, or attempted to state the events as they were already stated in the official Party historiography.

For example, N.A. Glagolev noted that Stalin "was very restrained in his manner" and was little known, and that Zinovyev supported him very actively. Then he noted that

---

15. This conference was recorded in shorthand.
16. RCPSMHD, f. 71, op. 1, d. 411.

it had not occurred to anybody what could happen in the future "if J.V. Stalin remains as General Secretary from here on in." Glagolev said that the Ukrainian delegation headed by Petrovskiĭ supported Stalin. No other candidates (Kuĭbyshev, Rudzutak, Dzerzhinskiĭ, Frunze) were proposed by this delegation at the meeting, and the other members of the Politburo (Zinovyev, Kamenev, Bukharin) could not compete with Stalin.[17]

S.O. Kotlyar declared that Stalin had "played the lamb" at the Thirteenth Party Congress, and also said that the youth (which he represented at the Congress) were literally deceived by the General Secretary. "We were so intoxicated, or, more precisely, fooled, that persons who suffered as a result of this history praised Stalin even in the [concentration] camps.[18]

Almost all who spoke (the majority of whom had suffered from Stalin's repressions) thought that, by the Thirteenth Congress, the outcome of the struggle between the General Secretary and Trotsky had already been predetermined. For example, Kotlyar declared at this conference that today (i.e., in the sixties), everyone asks, "Why was the letter that Vladimir Ilyich sent to the Twelfth Congress was read at the Thirteenth Congress? What happened? Why were they afraid to show this letter to the Twelfth Congress? After all, it was already known at that time that it existed."[19]

Kotlyar's answer to his own question reflects not merely his own understanding of the events, but that of the majority of the young people at the Congress. Kotlyar declared, "This

---

17. Ibid., sh. 14–16.
18. Ibid., sh. 23.
19. Ibid., sh. 21.

approach was taken in order to falsify history . . . because Stalin feared Trotsky. Trotsky was presented in a better light in Vladimir Ilyich's will than Stalin was."[20] Apparently at that time the majority of the Congress supported Stalin.

In the delegates' opinion, "Stalin saw that, according to the will, he [Trotsky] was his only rival. Further, Stalin was in the weaker position because Lenin said, in 1924 [?], that Stalin could not be General Secretary, since he acted rudely. So, during these months, Stalin readied his personnel to fight his rival Trotsky and to build up a ruling clique. But since Trotsky has an unsavory background . . . and showed what he was in Brest, and what role he played, and what he said during the discussion on the trade unions at the Tenth Congress, the only thing that built up was a great deal of dissatisfaction. The more so that Stalin professed he would no longer act rudely and would not do such things; though, afterwards, he did far worse things. . . ."[21]

Not everyone, of course, remembered the details of this Congress. For example, Verkhovykh, who addressed the conference, assured the participants that right after the opening of the Thirteenth Congress Krupskaya insisted that Lenin's will be read. He also claimed that the letter contained the character descriptions of other members of the Central Committee (Dzerzhinskii, Molotov, Kalinin).

M.A. Levkovich emphasized that Stalin was little known in the Party. (His role in the October revolution was particularly unknown—or, to be more precise, it was known for its insignificance). At the same time, Levkovich said that Stalin's oath of loyalty to Lenin in January 1924 made a

---

20. Ibid., sh. 22.
21. Ibid.

great impression on everyone. The Council of Elders, which had, as was its custom, predetermined the outcome of any talks about the will at the Congresses, played a major role in the struggle between Stalin and Trotsky.[22]

It is well known that when working with participants' memoirs or recorded memories, one is constantly faced with inaccuracies, contradictions, and so forth. These inaccuracies are sometimes due to faulty memory. For example, Trotsky made a number of inaccurate statements in his description of the October revolution only five years after the event. These inaccuracies were probably unintentional, though Soviet historiography usually maintained the opposite. The same may be said about the events connected to Lenin's will. In *My Life*, for example, in dealing with Stalin and the circumstances by which he was promoted General Secretary, Trotsky obviously confused the Tenth (1921) and Eleventh (1922) Party Congresses, saying that, in his character description of Stalin, Lenin had called him a cook who was fond of preparing spicy dishes.[23]

Nevertheless, Trotsky himself zealously noted the mistakes of those who inaccurately presented information concerning the history of Lenin's will. For example, he subjected Radek's testimony to strong criticism. Emil Ludwig recorded the following episode of the history of Lenin's will:

After Lenin's death we, 19 persons of the Central Committee, sat nervously, waiting to hear what the leader whom we lost would tell us from his coffin. Lenin's widow handed

22. Ibid., sh. 34–37.
23. Lev D. Trotsky, *Moya zhizn'. Opyt avtobiografii* (*My Life*). 2 vols. (Berlin: Granit, 1930).

his letter to us. Stalin read it. No one moved during the reading. When it came to Trotsky, the letter stated: "His non-Bolshevik past is not accidental." At this point Trotsky interrupted the reading and asked, "How is it said there?" The sentence was repeated. That was the only interruption that was heard during this solemn hour.

Commenting on this point, Trotsky wrote, ". . . Radek/ Ludwig's description . . . is false from beginning to end— in small and large, in insignificant and significant details." Then he affirmed, "To begin with, Lenin did not write the will two years before his death, as the author [Ludwig] affirms, but one year before. It was dated January 4, 1923; Lenin died on January 21, 1924. His political life was definitively broken off in March 1923." But then Trotsky makes an assertion that, in my opinion, is also wrong:

The first official proclamation of the will in the Kremlin took place, not at the meeting of the Central Committee, as Ludwig writes, but at the Council of Elders of the Thirteenth Party Congress on May 24, 1924. It was not Stalin, but Kamenev, as Permanent Chairman of the Central Party Institutions, who read the will.[24]

One further piece of testimony from Trotsky should be mentioned, in light of his claim that he heard first the will in 1924. Trotsky writes:

---

24. Trotsky, "Portrety revolutsionerov: Sbornik" ("Portraits of Revolutionaries: A Collection"), in Yurií G. Felshtinskií, ed., *Moskovski Rabochií (Moscow Worker)* (1991), pp. 267–268.

The so-called will was written in two stages separated by an interval of ten days: on December 25, 1922 and January 4, 1923. Only two people originally knew about the document: M. Volodicheva, the stenographer who took it down from dictation, and Lenin's wife, N. Krupskaya. While a shadow of hope for Lenin's recovery was still present, Krupskaya kept the document under lock and key. Shortly before the Thirteenth Congress, after Lenin's death, she delivered the will to the Secretariat of the Central Committee in order for it to be distributed to the Party Congress's attention, for which it was intended.

At this time the Party machinery was semi-officially in the hands of the "troika" (Zinovyev, Kamenev, Stalin), but in actuality it was in Stalin's hands. The "troika" was firmly opposed to the proclamation of the will at the Congress; it is not difficult to understand the motives. Krupskaya kept insisting. At this stage the dispute took place behind the scenes. The question was put off until the meeting of the Council of Elders, i.e., the leaders of the provincial delegations. At this point, the opposition members of the Central Committee as well as myself heard for the first time about the will. After agreeing not to take notes, Kamenev began to read the text. The mood of the audience was actually considerably tense. But, as far as one can recall, I would say that those who already knew the content of the document were much more agitated. The "troika" introduced, through one of the figurehead persons, a proposal that had been coordinated beforehand with the provincial leaders: the document should be read to separate delegations in closed meetings; in this case nobody was be allowed to take notes; it was forbidden to cite the will at the Plenum of the Congress. Krupskaya proved, with her soft persistence, that it would be a direct breach of Lenin's wishes to deny him the right to give his last advice to the Party. But the members of the Council of Elders, bound by factional discipline, remained indomitable: The "troika's" proposal was passed by an overwhelming majority.[25]

We will note that Trotsky was here more worried about refuting the contention about his non-Bolshevik past, which, in the Stalinists' opinion, had always been his hidden villainy and the basis of his mistakes since 1917. Correctly rejecting all this, Trotsky gave the above version of events concerning Lenin's will.

But Trotsky disagrees here with Boris Bazhanov, who paints a different picture:

> The Plenum took place in the meeting hall of the Presidium of the All-Russian Central Executive Committee. Kamenev was sitting in the small low platform at the chairman's table, and Zinovyev was sitting next to him. Close to them was a table at which I sat. (As usual, I was a secretary at the Plenum of the Central Committee.) The members of the Central Committee were sitting on the chairs in rows facing the platform. Trotsky was sitting in the third row at the end of the middle passage; Pyatakov and Radek sat next to him. Stalin was sitting on the right side of the platform facing a window and the platform so that the members of the Central Committee could not see his face, but I could observe him very well at all times.
>
> Kamenev opened the meeting and read Lenin's letter. Silence reigned. Stalin's face became morose and tense. Following the scenario that had been worked out previously, Zinovyev immediately took the floor:

---

25. Ibid., pp. 268–269.

"Comrades, you all know Ilyich's posthumous will, and each word of his is law for us. More than once we vowed to perform what Ilyich adjured for us; and you know very well that we will keep this vow. But there is a point on which we are happy to establish that Ilyich's apprehensions have not been justified. We were all witnesses of our common work during the last months, and, just like me, you could see with satisfaction that what Ilyich feared did not take place. I refer to our General Secretary and to the danger of disunity in the Central Committee." (I convey the general sense of the speech.)

Naturally, it was a lie. The members of the Central Committee knew very well that there was disunity in the Central Committee. Everyone was silent. Zinovyev offered to re-elect Stalin as General Secretary. Trotsky was silent, too, but he showed his extreme contempt for this whole comedy with vigorous facial expressions.

For his part, Kamenev convinced the members of the Central Committee to keep Stalin as General Secretary. As before, Stalin was looking out the window with clenched jaws and a tense face. His fate was being decided.

Since everyone was silent, Kamenev offered to decide the question by a vote: "Who is for keeping Comrade Stalin as General Secretary of the Central Committee? Who is against? Who abstains?" The vote was taken by a show of hands. I went over the rows and counted the votes, giving Kamenev only a total result. The majority voted for keeping Stalin, a small group supporting Trotsky were against this, and several persons abstained. (I didn't even note who these persons were, since I was occupied with counting hands, which I very much regret.)[26]

---

26. Boris Bazhanov, *Vospominaniya byvshego sekretariya Stalina* (*The Reminiscences of Stalin's Former Secretary*) (Infodizain, 1990), p. 106.

Who was right in this case, Bazhanov or Trotsky? Where and when did the reading of the will take place? On May 24, 1924, at the Plenum of the Central Committee; or on May 21, 1924, at the meeting of the Council of Elders? We have already seen that Trotsky often made mistakes when describing certain important events. For example, in his criticism of Radek/Ludwig, mentioned above, he made one of these factual errors, saying that Lenin had written the will (character descriptions) in two stages: on December 25, 1922, and on January 4, 1923.[27] In reality, he wrote it on December 24 and 25, 1922, and January 4, 1923. It was not only Krupskaya and the stenographer Volodicheva who knew about these notes, but also Fotieva and Alliluyeva. Trotsky wrote that he, together with other members of the opposition, first learned about the will before the Thirteenth Congress. This confession, made on December 31, 1932, in Prinkipo, confirms the idea stated above; namely, that to the end of his life, Trotsky never knew that Stalin and his cohorts had read the will in December 1922 and had withheld this information from him.

But we have not yet answered the question relating the divergence between Bazhanov and Trotsky as to where and when Lenin's will was read. To judge from the information given above, without considering Krupskaya's note to be a falsification, the events as a whole developed as Trotsky and Bazhanov presented them.

It seems to me that Bazhanov correctly related the course of events: as a record filed in the RCPSMHD testifies, the Plenum of the Central Committee of the Party took place on May 21. At this Plenum a resolution was adopted on

27. Trotsky, "Portrety revolutsionerov: Sbornik" ("Portraits of Revolutionaries: A Collection"), p. 268.

Kamenev's report in strict accordance with the Commission's May 19 decision.[28] Apparently Trotsky was correct when he wrote about the meeting of the Council of Elders of the Congress.

To judge from events at the Twelfth Congress, the meeting of the Council of Elders could have conceivably also taken place at the Thirteenth Congress, but if so, its agenda is unknown to us. At the same time, I discovered records of two provincial delegations meetings that reveal the manner of the "reading" of Lenin's will and the manner of the decision-making by delegations that were apparently subordinated to the will of the Council of Elders. These two records include the meetings' resolutions—first, of the delegations from the Volga and Central Industrial regions, dated May 25; and second, of the Ural, Siberian, Far East, Bashkir, and Vyatka delegations, dated May 26:

Resolution

Having been made aware of Lenin's unpublished notes and having exchanged opinions, the united meeting of the Ural, Siberian, Far-East, Bashkir, and Vyatka delegations at the Thirteenth Party Congress resolves:

1. To consider the inner-Party line followed by the Polit- buro of the Central Committee and Secretariat during the last year as correct and to try, at the elections of the new Central Committee, to provide solid Party leadership for the future in the spirit of Lenin's old tactics.

---

28. See page 82.

2. Taking into consideration that, despite the defects mentioned by Vladimir Ilyich, Comrade Stalin can cope better than anybody else with these gigantic, difficult, and complex tasks, which, in Lenin's absence, fall on the General Secretary of the Party; and taking into consideration also that the character description of Comrade Stalin was given as far back as the Twelfth Congress and that Lenin's apprehensions from times past about Comrade Stalin are not justified, consider it necessary that Comrade Stalin keep the post of General Secretary of the Party in the future.

Approved   Lashevich
                  M. Kharitonov

Kubyak[29]

*   *   *

Resolution
of the Meeting of the Thirteenth Party Congress's
delegations from the Volga and Central Industrial regions
25 May 1924

Having been made aware of Lenin's documents, the meeting of the delegations of the Volga and Central Industrial regions considers:

1. That V.I. Lenin's letters concerning personal character descriptions may have had the utmost importance at the time they were written and in the situation in which the Party found itself at the moment they were written, because of Lenin's illness.

---

29. RCPSMHD, f. 52, op. 1, d. 57, sh. 186.

2. The parts dealing with personal evaluations, the work of the Party, and, in particular, Party discussions, show that the leading group of the Central Committee, excepting Trotsky, quite correctly shaped the policy of the Party and was able to unite the whole Party around the Central Committee.

3. V.I. Lenin's apprehension that, due to his character, the General Secretary of the Party, Comrade Stalin, might abuse his power, has not been confirmed.

4. The Party's present position, due to the increase in the size of the Central Committee, which was done at the Twelfth Congress according to V.I. Lenin's directive; due to the Lenin Enrollment in the Party that strengthened it; and due to the results of Party discussion that united the Party on the basis of Leninism, protects the Party against the dangers to which V.I. Lenin drew its attention, and requires unconditional unity within the Central Committee on the basis of Leninism.

5. The parts of the letters containing personal character descriptions are not subject to proclamation at the Congress Plenum, in the press, or within the Party.

Chairman of the meeting: Philipp Goloshchekin

Representative of the
Nizhnií Novgorod delegation: N. Uglanov

   25/V 1924

      107 delegates attended the meeting.[30]

---

30. Ibid., sh. 183–184.

*   *   *

Minutes of the united meeting of the Ural, Siberian,
Far-East, Bashkir, and Vyatka delegations of the
Thirteenth Congress of the RCP(b)

Comrade Lashevich is elected as the Chairman who
reads V.I.'s unpublished notes.

Participating in the debate are Comrades Makarov,
Zaslavskií, Stanislav Kossior, Kharitonov, Lashevich, and
others.

After an exchange of opinions, the resolution (attached)
is read by Comrade Kubyak and put to vote. Results of
voting:

The first point is accepted by all votes but one abstention.
The second point is unanimously accepted.
The suggested corrections are rejected.

Chairman of the meeting: Lashevich
Secretary: M. Kharitonov
    N. Kubyak

Moscow, 26 May 1924[31]

As one can see from the documents, Stalin achieved what
he wanted. The fate of Lenin's letter had been determined
in the resolutions of the delegations: "The parts of the letters
containing personal character descriptions are not subject
to proclamation at the Congress Plenum, in the press, or
within the Party."

It is no mere chance that in the following month Viacheslav
Mikhailovich Molotov carefully collected information on the

---

31. Ibid., sh. 185.

possibility that information about Lenin's notes might seep to the provinces from which the delegates came. He was constantly informing Stalin about these results. At first everything was calm, but then disquieting news came from the Ukraine. First Kviring sent the following alarming telegram:

> *TOP SECRET*
> Copying forbidden
> CODED MESSAGE.

From Kharkov, sent on 19/VI, 1924, 16:30

Received by the Code Bureau of the Central Committee of the Russian Communist Party for decoding on 19/VI 1924, 19:10.

> Ref. No. 36/III

MOSCOW, CC RCP

Comrade STALIN.

Misunderstandings regarding the interpretation of the letters took place at Kharkov at the Party meetings. It was resolved to comment exclusively within the limits of the Congress delegation resolution, to which purpose the resolution was sent to the provincial committees.

Specially authorized comrades shall give the explanations at the Party cells.[32]

Approve urgently. NR 14/SH.

Secretary of the CC UCP[33]:   K V I R I N G

---

32. In pre-World War II Soviet Union, "cell" was the name used for a primary or local Party organization.

33. UCP = Ukrainian Communist Party.

Decoded on 19/6 1924, 20:10. Two copies were typed.

Signature   S. Chechulin.-[34]

The coded message was accompanied by the following text:

EXTRACTS FROM INSTRUCTIONS:

1. The coded telegram shall be kept only in the secret repositories.
2. After its use the coded message is to be returned to the Code Bureau of the Central Committee within a two-week period.
3. In references to coded telegrams it is forbidden to specify that the cited text was received by code, as well as to show the [reference] numbers of the coded messages.
4. An answer to a coded message must also be coded, the text of the coded message is to be drawn up briefly and clearly, [and] is to be written only in one copy, which is sent for coding.[35]

Then Kviring sent a more detailed message:

Comrade Stalin

Personal

It turned out that we had some problems with the letters in Kharkov: Grig[orii] Ivan[ovich] and Lebed spoke about them in their reports at the regional meetings (over 2,000 memb[ers] of the Party participated in each of them). In my report at the third region (on the same day and

---

34. RCPSMHD, f. 52, op. 1, d. 57, sh. 191.
35. Ibid.

hour) I didn't think it appropriate to speak about the letters at such a wide meeting.

As a result, rumors are spread: if one doesn't speak, others speak. Everything would be all right; nobody talks about Lebed's report because he skillfully stated his case, not giving too much importance to these letters.

It took Grig[orii] Iv[anovich] half an hour to read the letters, and he called these "Lenin's spiritual will." A number of statements came to me and to the Politburo about the unsuccessful manner in which the letters were presented, which left the impression that Lev David[ovich Trotsky] was the only member of the Central Committee. I think that our people overrated the failure; in any case they believe that the opposition uses it strongly.

Our Politburo decided to speak about the letter only at the Party cells, and only to specially entrusted comrades, and only within the limits of our delegation's resolution.

We decided to give such a directive to the provincial committees and requested your sanction. It is necessary to do this, otherwise there will be confusion.

There are as yet no complications in the provinces.

Greetings,

E. Kviring

19/VI 24[36]

The Society of Old Bolsheviks also requested the will. On May 30 the Society sent the following letter to Stalin:

---

36. Ibid., sh. 189-190.

SECRETARY OF THE CC RCP(b)

Comrade S T A L I N

Dear Comrade,
The Society of Old Bolsheviks requests that a copy of Lenin's "will" be read to all the delegations of the Thirteenth Congress of the Russian Communist Party.

The Society of Old Bolsheviks considers it necessary to acquaint our members with the content of this document that gave rise to all kinds of rumors, which undoubtedly distorted to a certain extent the content of this historical document.

The "will" should be read at a closed meeting and only in the presence of the Society's actual members

Secretary of the Bureau:
Mikhaílov [Signature: L. Mikhaílov][37]

We don't know whether the Old Bolsheviks received the information, but, in general, Stalin could feel at ease. In a note to Stalin, Molotov said that "*no announcements about misunderstandings concerning the letter* [the will] *have been heard anywhere in the RCP.*"[38]

Thus, at last, by the spring or summer of 1924 Stalin collected, it seems, everything that was dictated by Lenin in late 1922 and early 1923 and made it secret and inaccessible to most Party members. At the same time, one cannot still say with certainty that everything published on this question in Lenin's *Complete Works* fully reflects everything that

---

37. Ibid., sh. 187.
38. Ibid., sh. 188 obverse.

Lenin dictated. As we have seen, some parts were falsified, and sometimes even deleted. The following confirms this.

Lenin's final dictations, from December 1922 through early March 1923, were the subject of a study in articles by V.I. Starzev and S.V. Voronkova. (Voronkova took into consideration only Lenin's articles from December 23, 1922 through December 28, 1923). Both articles are of particular importance. Though not working in archives with Lenin's original materials, Voronkova nevertheless made some important observations. Considering each text of a dictation by Lenin as a "unit," Voronkova discovered the following. In May 1924, Krupskaya produced 13 separate notes. Since part of the works dictated by Lenin had been already published (i.e., the note about the Workers' and Peasants' Inspection and Sukhanov), and since Lenin's sister, Mariya Ilyinichna, possessed the letter on the national problem, it was possible to count the number of notes that Krupskaya delivered.

Then Voronkova writes: "the notes from December 24–25, 1922 and January 4, 1923, which included the personal character descriptions of several members of the Central Committee, were not published." She maintains that the notes made on December 23, 24, 25, 26, and 29, January 4, as well as two notes for the article "On Our Revolution" and five texts of the article "How We Shall Reorganize the Workers' and Peasants' Inspection," constitute the 13 notes. In her opinion, this total did not include "Granting Legislative Functions to the State Planning Commission" (which was delivered later, in June 1923), "Pages from the Diary," and "Better Less, But Better." In all, there were approximately 20 dictations (taking into consideration that the last article most likely comprised several dictations). Voronkova found that, according to the material in volume 45 of Lenin's *Complete Works*, "29 notes are each distinguished as a unit of text by a special dating, title, and graphical analysis." Furthermore, her results showed that according to the diary of the deputy secretaries and the "Biochronicle," the number of dictations was even higher.[39]

Therefore more research should be carried out in order to establish (if possible) the possibility that a part of Lenin's dictations were deleted. In particular, Valentinov states that when Lenin arrived in Moscow in October 1922, he searched for but did not find some of his notes in his Kremlin office. But there is one more piece of evidence that some of Lenin's notes were not kept as carefully and as secretly as usual. Sometimes notes written by him were discovered quite unexpectedly.

To cite an example, the authors of a book about Lenin's Kremlin office sorted out the items in his flat when it became accessible in 1954, after Stalin's death. They wrote, "When we were first introduced to the flat we noted an original briefcase that had been found in the closed part of a sideboard in the corridor near Lenin's room. This brown briefcase of thick leather with eight numbered partitions was locked and fastened by straps. It looked quite new and empty. A few days later one of the employees of the museum looked inside it for some reason and extracted slim sheets from the depth of its partitions. On one of the sheets was written: 'To be opened only by Vladimir Ilyich (according to his instruction)

---

39. S.V. Voronkova, "Nekotorye problemy istochnikovedeniya otechestvennoĭ istorii, XIX–XX vekov" ("Some Problems of the Source Study of the Country History, XIX–XX Centuries") *Istoriya SSSR* (*History of the USSR*), 1989, no. 6, p. 41.

or by Nadezhda Konstantinovna.' On the other: 'On the Workers' and Peasants' Inspection, January 9 and 13'."[40]

The employees of the museum mentioned this to Volodicheva and Dridzo, who confirmed that Krupskaya kept Lenin's last letters and articles in a briefcase. They then understood how important their discovery was.[41]

---

40. L. Kunetskaya, K. Mashtakova, *Vstrecha s Leninym: Po materialam muzeya "Kabinet i Kvartira V.I. Lenina v Kremle"* (*Meetings with Lenin: Based on the Material from the Museum "V.I. Lenin's Office and Flat in the Kremlin"*) (Moscow, 1987), pp. 262–263.

41. Ibid., p. 263.

Six

The Max Eastman Affair

Often seen in the lobby of the Thirteenth Party Congress, held at the end of May 1924, one man stood out from the others. It was not only his Western clothes that made him conspicuous. Some of the delegates had met him at the Fourth Comintern Congress; and now that journalist with a guest card boldly approached various delegates, talked with Trotsky, and leafed through heaps of Party literature piled on the tables.

A year later, in May 1925, his name often appeared in the columns of European newspapers. He was Max Eastman, a member of the American Communist Party, a journalist who spoke Russian fluently. In the summer of 1925 he was the object of many discussions at Politburo meetings because of his book, *Since Lenin Died*, which had been published in London and Paris and had become a political bestseller.[1]

---

1. Max Eastman, *Since Lenin Died* (London: Labour Publishing, 1925).

Eastman did not conceal his friendly attitude toward Trotsky. He wrote that the Russian Communist Party was being rent by inner-Party struggles that had begun during Lenin's lifetime. That was nothing new; but he also mentioned that the controversy was raging around Lenin's documents. Eastman asserted that the top leaders of the Party—Stalin, Kamenev, and Zinovyev—had held Lenin's political will under wraps without informing the broad Party membership about it. The news of Lenin's "Letter to the Congress" first reached the West in 1923. A very distorted version of this letter had first been published in the *Socialist Bulletin*. Now Eastman offered a more accurate version.

Trotsky was the first to respond to the appearance of Eastman's book. *Pravda* (May 9, 1925) carried a message by Jackson, editor-in-chief of the *Sunday Worker* (London), and Trotsky's reply to it. Jackson's message ran as follows:

Moscow, The Kremlin.

Comrade Trotsky.
    Eastman's book is widely quoted in the bourgeois press. You are described as the victim of intrigue. The idea is being raised that you favor democracy and free trade.

Trotsky cabled in reply that he did not know anything about the book's contents and stressed:

Like all Party members, I regard the system of the dictatorship of the proletariat and foreign trade monopoly as part and parcel of socialist construction.

Stalin took some time to reply. Having studied the book in Russian translation, he transformed his reply into a major political action. A platform was being elaborated under his guidance throughout the summer of 1925; its purpose was to explain why the Party had not been supplied with information about Lenin's political will.

As early as the spring of 1925 Stalin had started preparations for destroying his own Kamenev-Stalin-Zinovyev bloc, with which he had managed to vanquish Trotsky back in 1923–1924. There had been clashes among the bloc's members even prior to this. According to Tomskií, back in 1924, during the May Day celebrations, Stalin had snubbed Zinovyev in the presence of their close friends, at his country-house, for his attempts to play first fiddle. (Having been carried away by his leading position at the Comintern, Zinovyev appointed Stalin his deputy without having consulted him.) However, although the bloc was on its last legs, it still existed, for its members were unanimous in their hatred of Trotsky.

In the summer of 1925 Stalin involved Zinovyev in a new campaign of criticism leveled against Trotsky—thus demonstrating for Zinovyev and Kamenev what the future might hold in store for them should they not obey the General Secretary's orders. Stalin set himself the task of making Trotsky renounce the views he had held in 1923–1924 regarding Lenin's will, and of making him dissociate himself from Eastman. He endeavored to make Trotsky compromise himself so that any resistance on his part would be tantamount to political suicide and thus impossible. Moreover, by making Trotsky dissociate himself from Eastman, Stalin hoped to put an end to all doubts among the leadership of the Communist Parties in the West, convincing them that he, not Trotsky, was right.

It is possible today, by analyzing the entire set of documents pertaining to 1925, which are now available to researchers, to reveal the principles by which the Stalinist school of historical falsification operated.

While preparing documents for the Eastman affair, Stalin's apparatus manifested a truly infernal foresight. The main document in this matter, a memorandum for the Politburo, formally seemed to be logical and convincing, so much so that future historians, ignorant of the details, could be fully convinced that Stalin was completely right. However, unpublished correspondence on that issue has been preserved, and it testifies, as we shall see, that everything published by Trotsky on this issue had in reality been written by Stalin's group.

The history of Eastman's acquaintance with Trotsky reveals the far from simple nature of the relations and goals pursued by each. Since Eastman played a prominent role in the destiny of Lenin's will, more details should be supplied about him. *Who's Who in America* offers the following information about him:

Eastman, Max (Forrester), author, editor; b. Canandaigua, N.Y., Jan. 4, 1883; s. Samuel Elijah and Annis Bertha (Ford) E.; A.B., Williams, 1905; studied Columbia, 1907-10. . . . Assistant in Philosophy, Columbia, 1907-10, associate, 1911; engaged in lecturing. . . . Organized first Men's League for Woman Suffrage in U.S., 1910. . . .[2]

---

2. *Who's Who in America: A Biographical Dictionary of Notable Living Men and Women*, vol. 31 (Chicago: A.N. Marquis Company, 1960), p. 836.

Eastman's own works point out that he joined the Socialist Party of the U.S.A. in 1911, was editor of the *Masses* journal (1913–1917), and later of the *Liberator* (1918–1922). The March 1918 issue of the *Liberator* carried John Reed's article, "Bolsheviks' Triumph." *The Liberator* also published materials about Lenin and Trotsky. More often than not, people judge Eastman by his autobiographical works. However, if one takes into account both his own opinion of himself and of his actions, one might draw the following conclusions.

Eastman was undoubtedly a well educated and enterprising person and a capable journalist. He went to Moscow after he had joined the Worker's Party (Communist Party) of the U.S.A. in 1921. He spent two years in Russia, mastered Russian during the winter of 1922–1923, and was well received in circles close to the Comintern, which were close to Trotsky. This reception was facilitated by his second marriage to Yelena Krylenko, the sister of a prominent Russian Bolshevik who was later appointed People's Commissar of Justice of Russia.

It should be noted that in the initial years of Soviet power, three prominent Americans made their contribution to Russian history. One of them, John Reed, wrote a book about the October 1917 coup,[3] and the other two, Armand Hammer and Max Eastman, who, like Reed, were loyal to communist ideals, were also businessmen. Their actions had much in common. Armand Hammer, a physician by profession, after having become a Comintern agent, was consolidating his success in the business sphere. Having ob-

---

3. John Reed, *Ten Days That Shook the World* (New York: Boni and Liveright, 1919).

tained permission for opening Soviet Russia's first concession
with a foreigner, he left for the U.S.A. in the autumn of
1922. It took Hammer only a year to start his business in
Russia, which later brought him world renown. Hammer's
success was based on Lenin's personal support—Lenin had
granted an audience to him.[4]

Eastman, the journalist who had arrived in Russia in
September 1922, was young and no less enterprising than
Hammer. He managed to establish contacts with a leader
who, as Lenin's associate, was engaged in settling important
problems of Russia's development. Lev Trotsky was Max
Eastman's ideal in those years, as the latter wrote later.
Hoping for popularity, glory, and money, Eastman decided
to write a book about Trotsky; for Trotsky was second only
to Lenin in importance among the Russian Communist Party
leaders, and his name was widely known in the world.

On November 5, 1922 the Fourth Comintern Congress
opened in Moscow. On that day, Dr. A. Kozhevnikov, who
kept notes of Lenin's case history, wrote, "In the morning
he had a fit of clonospasms and paralysis."[5] However, Lenin
soon felt better, and on November 13 made his last public
address at the Comintern Congress. However, even then
many people believed that Trotsky would soon take Lenin's
place.

---

4. Jerrold L. Schecter and Yuri Buranov, "Documents tie Hammer
to communists. Declassified files show industrialist and his father aided
party." We (a weekly supplement to the newspaper Izvestiya), June 15–
28, 1992.

5. "Dnevnik dezhurnogo vracha V.I. Lenina v 1922–1923 gg." ("The
Diary of V.I. Lenin's Doctor on Duty, 1922–1923"), Voprosy istorii KPSS
(The Questions of History of the CPSU), 1992, no. 9, p. 42.

Eastman met Trotsky at that Congress. In 1925 Eastman wrote a preface to Trotsky's book, in which he related his first encounters with Trotsky in very reserved terms. Trotsky paid him in the same coin in a document carried by *L'humanité*. As it transpired later, each of them took his own view of the meaning and purpose of their acquaintance. At that time Eastman was writing a book about Trotsky's younger years, but Trotsky must not have taken much interest in Eastman's popularization of his personality abroad. Trotsky was more attracted by the opportunity to tell the West in a roundabout way, via Eastman, what he could not directly tell in Russia regarding the struggle around Lenin's will.

In August 1923 Trotsky, keeping his word, gave Eastman a letter of recommendation, which enabled him to expand his contacts with Bolshevik leaders. The will was read to individual delegations of the Thirteenth Party Congress in May 1924. On the 26th of that month Trotsky made his speech without ever mentioning Lenin's will. It was on that day that Trotsky informed Eastman about the contents of Lenin's document. It should be noted, however, that Eastman did not receive a copy of Lenin's will from Trotsky. Many years later Eastman wrote that, "Trotsky confided in me by telling me about the strictly guarded secret of Lenin's will." But he never said that Trotsky had supplied him with a copy of that document.[6] Moreover, Eastman mentioned that Boris Suvarin and Rosmer, members of the Comintern Execu-

---

6. V.V. Shvetsov, "Lev Trotskiĭ i Maks Istmen: istoriya odnoi politicheskoi dryzhby" ("Lev Trotsky and Max Eastman: the Story of One Political Friendship"), *Novaya i noveĭshaya istoriya* (*New and the Newest History*), 1990, no. 6, p. 149.

tive, had supplied him with "additional information" on the issue.

Immediately after Eastman's book was published, Trotsky informed the Politburo about all his contacts with Eastman. He stressed at the same time that he did not know Eastman very well.[7] He wrote that he had met Eastman "as an American Communist at one of the first Congresses of the Comintern," and that "three or four years" ago Eastman had asked him for assistance for a biography he was writing. (Indeed, Eastman had visited and interviewed Trotsky's relatives and school friends for *Lev Trotsky: A Portrait of a Youth.*) Trotsky also pointed out that he had agreed to supply information about himself, but that he did not intend to read the manuscript before publication. Trotsky's memo must not have disturbed Stalin's peace of mind. However, Trotsky later supplied more information that proved to be of substantial importance to Stalin.

It transpired that Eastman's contacts with Trotsky continued even after the book's publication, although Trotsky assured Stalin that "the last time" he had seen Eastman was "over a year and a half" ago, and that he knew nothing about the American's intention to write a book about the discussions within the Party. Trotsky pointed out that he had not given the documents to Eastman, but the latter spoke Russian fluently and had a wide circle of acquaintances among Soviet Communists.[8]

Having read a Russian translation of Eastman's book (and having sent copies of this translation to Politburo members), Stalin made preparations to discuss it at an extended

---

7. RCPSMHD, f. 325, op. 1, d. 417, sh. 28,107.
8. Ibid.

meeting of the Politburo on June 18, 1925, at which he once again leveled criticisms against Trotsky. He launched a vigorous propaganda campaign to promulgate his own interpretation of the events around Lenin's will.

A special memo was read at the meeting, in which Stalin pointed out that on May 8, 1925, the Politburo received Trotsky's statement about his correspondence with the editorial office of the *Sunday Worker* on Eastman's *Since Lenin Died*. After describing, on the basis of Trotsky's memo, the further course of events, Stalin declared that he was stunned not so much by Eastman's statement that "Russia is governed by an irresponsible handful of usurpers and liars" or by Trotsky's distortion of the latest Party discussion, as by Trotsky's role in connection with the publication of Eastman's book.[9]

Stalin did not demand any explanations from Trotsky on the problems dealt with in the book. He simply "asked" him politely to explain the obvious distortions of facts, as described by Eastman. The General Secretary's calculation was simple enough. There were many inaccuracies in Eastman's book; so by confirming this fact, Trotsky would prove that Eastman's book was of no value. However, this was not Stalin's main goal; Stalin wanted to obtain from Trotsky a personal statement that would deny his own previous assertions from 1923 and 1924 concerning the destiny of Lenin's documents. And it was precisely those assertions that Eastman advocated.

Stalin demanded that Trotsky proclaim certain of Eastman's statements "slanderous." For example, in the second chapter of his book, Eastman pointed out that in 1923 the

9. RCPSMHD, f. 17, op. 3, d. 507, sh. 13.

RCP Politburo had objected to publishing Lenin's article on the Workers' and Peasants' Inspection. As we have seen, Trotsky had stated this in a number of official documents; but now, "forgetting" that this assertion was Trotsky's, not Eastman's, Stalin demanded that Trotsky proclaim this to be "slander." Stalin wrote:

> I believe . . . that he [Trotsky] cannot help but remember that, first, Lenin's plan, discussed by him in that article, was not discussed substantively at that time; that, second, a meeting of the Politburo was then held in reference to Lenin's well known passage about a possible split in the CC—words that might evoke perplexity in Party organizations. Comrade Trotsky cannot help but know that the Politburo then decided to send a special letter of the Orgburo and Politburo of the CC explaining that Lenin's article should not be grounds for fears of a potential split in the CC. Comrade Trotsky cannot help but know that the decisions regarding the publication of Lenin articles, as well as the publication of the letters of Orgburo and Politburo members concerning the absence of any split within the CC, were adopted unanimously; and that the allegations that the decision concerning the publication of Lenin's letter was adopted under Comrade Trotsky's pressure are ridiculous nonsense.[10]

By thus giving the lie to Eastman's objective presentation of Trotsky's stand on the issue of Lenin's article about the Workers' and Peasants' Inspection, Stalin demanded that Trotsky also admit that the fuss around the article on the national problem was also of a slanderous nature. On this

---

10. Ibid.

point, Stalin caught Eastman red-handed, since Eastman, for lack of accurate information, had distorted the facts by stating that the article had not been read at the Congress.

After pointing out that the article had indeed been read, though not published, Stalin stressed that the decision not to publish was not his own. He painstakingly recreated the whole picture:

> . . . The CC could not help but take into account that Lenin's sister, Mariya Ulyanova, who had Lenin's article, did not deem its publication necessary. This was explained by Lenin's personal secretary, Comrade Fotieva, in a special document dated 16 April 1923 in reply to Stalin's offer to publish the article: "Mariya Ilyinichna said," Fotieva wrote, "that if there was no direct order from V.I. to publish this article, it should not be published; though she thinks members of the Congress should be informed about it. . . ." And Fotieva added her own opinion, saying that "V.I. did not consider this article ready for publication."[11]

Having stated all that, Stalin demanded that any other interpretation of the events be regarded as slanderous.

Along with Stalin, Zinovyev was also among the first to criticize Eastman's book; and later the French communists, in particular Cachin, followed suit. Each of them contributed to the general conclusion that the book was of a "slanderous" nature, but in each case the critic pursued his own individual goals, determined by the alignment of forces in the struggle for power in the Party. Stalin's stand was determined by his desire to conceal permanently Lenin's last works and

---

11. Ibid.

to keep the Party ignorant of their contents.

Trotsky found himself in a paradoxical situation. All CC members knew what he had written in his letters of 1923. On the basis of those letters, Eastman was trying to prove that Trotsky had insisted on publishing Lenin's works, whereas Stalin had been opposed to such. And now Stalin, pretending they were nonexistent, had cast aside all of Trotsky's letters written in 1923 on that subject and demanded that Trotsky proclaim Eastman's interpretation of his position to be "slander." As a result, by proclaiming Eastman a slanderer, Trotsky admitted that he himself was also a slanderer.

To "facilitate" the task of Trotsky's political suicide, Stalin made use of Eastman's purely factual mistakes. For instance, Eastman wrote that the Twelfth Party Congress was not familiarized with Lenin's letter on the national problem, although in reality this letter had been read to the delegations. He also erroneously asserted that Lenin wished to appoint Trotsky chairman of the Council of People's Commissars in September 1922; although in reality at that time Trotsky refused to act as one of the vice-chairmen.

Stalin was again trying to convince the Party leadership that it was he, not Trotsky, who was prepared to inform the Party of the ideas Lenin expressed in the last period of his life. At the same time, offended by Eastman's scornful assessment of him, Zinovyev believed, and not without reason, that Eastman was nothing more than a mouthpiece for Trotsky's ideas. By taking part in the debates around Eastman's book, Zinovyev hoped to exclude both Trotsky and Stalin from the leading role in the Party. Further developments, connected with statements by Kamenev and Zinovyev at the Fourteenth Party Congress and the formation of a "new opposition" to Stalin, proved that this was indeed Zinovyev's goal. The Max Eastman affair was of great importance in preparations for an open struggle against Stalin.

Zinovyev studied Eastman's book all through the summer. His personal copy of the translation, in which he left a great number of notes, has been preserved.[12] I have examined his notes in detail. With red and blue pencil he underscored the passages he found most offensive to himself personally, as well as passages that seemed to confirm his suspicions that, by writing the book, Eastman had in fact fulfilled Trotsky's commission. Zinovyev endeavored to discover in Eastman's book ideas that Trotsky had expressed in his own works. In chapter 1, "Lenin and Trotsky," Zinovyev noted the following sentence: "It is well known among Trotsky's friends that he received a letter from Lenin's wife some days after Lenin died, reminding him of their early friendship in London, and assuring him that Lenin's feelings towards him had never changed from then until the day of his death."[13] He underscored that sentence and inscribed the letter "T," i.e., Trotsky. It should be noted that not many people knew about the letter Krupskaya wrote to Trotsky, and it was only the addressee who could have told Eastman about it.

In chapter 2, "The Anti-Bonaparte Fraction," Zinovyev wrote the word "Radek" next to the following sentence: "He [Trotsky] does not know how to manipulate men. He has no impulse to do it. He never thinks of it." "Radek" was also written next to one more sentence: "And with a quixotic objectiveness which is far harder to understand than cal-

12. RCPSMHD, f. 324, op. 1, d. 312. The Russian version of Eastman's book is called *After Lenin's Death*.

13. Ibid., sh. 5; Eastman, *Since Lenin Died*, p. 13.

culating ambition, he declined Lenin's proposal that he should become the head of the Soviet Government. . . ."[14]

Zinovyev was also occupied with collecting material that would compromise Stalin's group. Thus, he drew five longitudinal lines in red pencil on the margin of the page next to the following quote from Lenin's article, "How We Shoulde Reorganize the Workers' and Peasants' Inspection":

"The People's Commissariat of Worker's and Peasant's Inspection [Kuíbyshev] does not enjoy at the present time a shadow of authority. Everybody knows that a worse organised institution than this one does not exist, and that under the present conditions you can ask nothing whatever of this institution."[15]

Eastman wrote that this "ingenious secretary," who became People's Commissar of the Worders' and Peasants' Inspection, and who was also People's Commissar of the Central Control Commission, obstructed the implementation of Lenin's ideas. Kuíbyshev, as Stalin's firm supporter, also served as an obstacle to the plans of Zinovyev's group. That is why Zinovyev was interested in the clashes between Trotsky and Kuíbyshev that took place in 1923, and which had been described by Eastman. This is what Eastman wrote about their clash:

The Politburo was discussing changes in the organisation of the Red Army, designed to weaken the power of Trotsky. Trotsky frankly stated to them that the real motive of their

---

14. RCPSMHD, f. 324, op. 1, d. 312, sh. 9–10; Eastman, pp. 17–18.
15. RCPSMHD, f. 324, op. 1, d. 312, sh. 15; Eastman, p. 24.

act had nothing in common with the motives officially announced. And Kuibeshev answered him just as frankly:

"We consider it necessary to fight you, and we cannot declare you an enemy; that is why we are compelled to resort to such methods."[16]

This was true, and Zinovyev believed that the classified material on this issue (Trotsky had written about this matter in a letter to the CC in 1923) could only have been supplied to Eastman by Trotsky. True, Eastman admitted that he had learned about this from the *Sotzialisticheskii Vestnik* (*Socialist Bulletin*), not from Trotsky; but Zinovyev did not believe this, since he put two question marks next to those words in the text.

Zinovyev's attention was especially attracted to Eastman's admission that:

"I met him [Trotsky] for a moment accidentally; I told him then that I knew about 'The Testament of Lenin,' and he told me to regard whatever I knew as an 'absolute secret.' That has been an additional reason for my delay in writing this article."[17]

Here Zinovyev wrote: "But you did not inform the CC about it."[18] Naturally, Zinovyev here referred to Trotsky, who, though he had reported on his contacts with Eastman in detail in his memo to the Politburo, had not mentioned a word about this particular conversation with Eastman.

The chapter on Lenin's will, "The Testament of Lenin,"

---

16. RCPSMHD, f. 324, op. 1, d. 312, sh. 16; Eastman, p. 26.
17. RCPSMHD, f. 324, op. 1, d. 312, sh. 17; Eastman, p. 26n.
18. RCPSMHD, f. 324, op. 1, d. 312, sh. 17.

dealt exclusively with the contents of Lenin's documents and the methods by which Stalin's group had tried to conceal them. Eastman quite justly pointed out that "Lenin evidently knew the drift of things in the Central Committee during those last months. And he had the intention to correct it at the forthcoming convention of the party." Eastman was also right in asserting that Lenin realized "that he might drop out of the scene at any moment," and that was why "he wrote a letter to the party, to be read at that convention."[19]

Eastman wrote that Krupskaya, however, in the hopes that Lenin would recuperate, did not present the will to the Twelfth Congress. Eastman's interpretation of what happened next also seems to be quite realistic. "And at the next convention (May, 1924)," he wrote, "the machine organised by Stalin and Zinoviev was already strong enough to defy the last will and testament of Lenin." He explained his idea in a footnote: "They [the Central Committee] decided that it might be read and explained privately to the delegates— kept within the bureaucracy, that is to say—but not put before the party for discussion, as Lenin directed."[20]

Eastman also wrote about the results of the vote at the CC Plenum on whether or not to discuss the matter at the Congress: 30 votes against and 10 in favor.[21] "Thus," Eastman concludes, "one of the most solemn and carefully weighed

---

19. Ibid., sh. 19; Eastman, p. 28.

20. RCPSMHD, f. 324, op. 1, d. 312; Eastman, p. 28 and 28n.

21. It should be noted that the record of proceedings of the discussion of that issue at the Plenary Meeting, held on May 21, 1924, is missing from the Russian Center for the Preservation and Study of Modern History Documents. The voting is mentioned in Boris Bazhanov's booklet, *Vospominaniya byvshego sekretariya Stalina* (*Reminiscences of Stalin's Former Secretary*) (Infodizain, 1990), p. 106.

utterances that ever came from Lenin's pen, was sup-
pressed—in the interests of 'Leninism'—by that triumvirate
of 'Old Bolsheviks,' Stalin, Zinoviev and Kamenev, who
govern the Russian Communist Party."[22]

Meanwhile, no matter how important Eastman's general
political conclusions were, no less important was the publication—the first publication—of a detailed account of
Lenin's will. The question arose: To what extent did it correspond to the original? Assuring the reader that he discussed
the authentic document, Eastman added the following note
to the summary of the will:

> The reader can rely absolutely upon the phrases from
> this letter which I have placed in quotation marks. They
> were verbally agreed upon by three responsible Commu-
> nists in Russia, whom I interviewed separately and who
> had all recently read the letter and committed its vital
> phrases to memory.[23]

This is what Eastman wrote:

> What does the letter say about these Old Bolsheviks?
> Of Stalin, it says that he has concentrated too much power
> in his hands, and it demands that he be removed from
> his dominating position as secretary of the party. It
> criticises his character as "too brutal."[24]

---

22. RCPSMHD, f. 324, op. 1, d. 312, sh. 19; Eastman, pp. 28–29.
23. RCPSMHD, f. 324, op. 1, d. 312, sh. 21; Eastman, pp. 30n–31n.
24. RCPSMHD, f. 324, op. 1, d. 312, sh. 20; Eastman, p. 29.

Eastman believed that Lenin's negative opinion of the General Secretary, Zinovyev, Kamenev, and Bukharin was drawn into even sharper relief by his statement that:

> Trotsky, in spite of his "too great self-confidence," is "a devoted revolutionist," and "the outstanding member of the Central Committee."

Eastman asserted that those were the opening words of Lenin's will, which was not true.[25] In reality, Lenin began "The Letter to the Congress" (dictated on December 24) with a general discussion of a possible threat of split in the Party, not with the "statement" that Trotsky was "a devoted revolutionist," as Eastman wrote. Interestingly, Lenin's statement about a possible clash between Stalin and Trotsky is not mentioned in Eastman's book.

Having pointed out, in his memo to the CC Plenum, all the mistakes in Eastman's book, Stalin was nevertheless compelled to remain silent about the contents of the will. Had he mentioned the contents, he would have had to have spoken about their substance; whereas, according to the decision of the Twelfth Congress, the contents of the will were not to be reproduced or discussed. Moreover, even the CC was powerless to revise that decision; it could only recommend that the issue be discussed at the next Party Congress. Thus, the Bolshevik tradition of extreme secrecy had simply absurd consequences: it became impossible even to point out obvious mistakes in the version of Lenin's document that had been unexpectedly published. For the same reason, all other Party leaders mentioned by Lenin in Eastman's

---

25. RCPSMHD, f. 324, op. 1, d. 312, sh. 21; Eastman, p. 30.

interpretation of the "Letter to the Congress"—Kamenev, Zinovyev, Pyatakov, and Bukharin—were forced to keep mum. (Bukharin had probably received the greatest dose of Eastman's criticism.)

Eastman wrote that Lenin described his associates in the following way: "Of Zinoviev and Kamenev it says just one thing: 'Their retreat[26] in October [1917] was not accidental'."[27] Further, with reference to Lenin's letter on their "retreat,"[28] Eastman went on:

> There were, in fact, two retreats at two different times, and Lenin characterised Zinoviev and Kamenev the first time as "strike-breakers" and "traitors," and the second time as "unbelievers," "waverers," "doubters," "deserters," "strike-breakers," and surrenderers to the bourgeoisie. The first retreat was immediately before the revolution of October, the second was immediately after it. That Lenin so judged these men, throughout the most critical days in the life of the party, had been by common consent forgotten. Their ability and prestige were needful to him, and neither of them ever opposed him upon a vital question again. Faced with the probability of his own death, however, Lenin saw fit to remind the party of that incident, and declare that their behaviour above characterised was "not accidental."[29]

---

26. As Eastman explains, the Russian word for "retreat" also means "apostasy."

27. Eastman, p. 29.

28. This letter is published as Appendix III in Eastman, pp. 137–140.

29. RCPSMHD, f. 324, op. 1, d. 312, sh. 20; Eastman, pp. 29–30.

According to Eastman, Lenin also said that "of the younger men the two most promising were Bucharin and Pitiakov [sic]. He did not qualify his praise of Pitiakov—who has stood with Trotsky throughout this crisis."[30] Here, too, Zinovyev could not help but note Eastman's obvious tendentiousness; for, in actuality, apart from praising Pyatakov, Lenin also said that he showed "too much zeal for administrating and the administrative side of the work to be relied upon in a serious political matter."[31]

I shall quote two excerpts for you to see the difference in the way Lenin and Eastman characterized Bukharin. Any commentary will be superfluous. This is what Lenin wrote:

Bukharin is not only a most valuable and major theorist of the Party; he is also rightly considered the favorite of the whole Party, but his theoretical views can be classified as fully Marxist only with great reserve, for there is something scholastic about him (he has never made a study of dialectics, and, I think, never fully understood it).[32]

Whereas Eastman interpreted Lenin's text in the following way:

His praise of Bucharin he did qualify in a very damaging way. Bucharin's prestige rests, by about one-half, upon his personal popularity. Revolutionary self-denial and devotion and courage and simplicity of life, are the causes of it. The other half of his prestige rests upon a supposed

---

30. Eastman, p. 30.
31. Lenin, *Polnoe Sobranie Sochinenii*, vol. 45, p. 345; *Collected Works*, vol. 36, p. 595.
32. Ibid.

theoretic mastery of the Marxian philosophy. Bucharin has written a book about Historic Materialism, which is at once so scholarly in appearance, and so utterly undigested and confusing to the brain, that most people are willing to concede his mastery of Marxism in order to avoid having to read and study this book. What Lenin said about Bucharin is that he "does not understand the Marxian dialectic"—which means that he does not know how to think with the method of Lenin—and that he is scholastic. "His head is full of books," is about the expression that Lenin used.[33]

Meanwhile, Stalin had a private meeting in which he, along with Bukharin and Rykov, who had joined in the anti-Eastman campaign, instructed Trotsky to write a denunciation of Eastman's book. After this meeting, on July 23, 1925, Trotsky wrote two letters, to Stalin and Krupskaya.

In his letter to the General Secretary, he expressed his thoughts about where his statement should be published, saying he would prefer to publish it abroad. "The more dryly and calmly I disavow Eastman's book *as one of no political importance, the better.*" [Italics added.] Regarding Eastman's interpretation of the will, Trotsky wrote:

One must be either an idiot or criminal to raise a clamor around the "document," for it has lost any meaning as a result of the course of events. If Eastman's book is to be discussed in a militant tone, then it is perfectly clear that it is necessary to concentrate more energetically and resolutely on that central and most "sensational" point.[34]

---

33. RCPSMHD, f. 324, op. 1, d. 312, sh. 20–21; Eastman, p. 30.
34. RCPSMHD, f. 325, op. 1, d. 417, sh. 60.

In his letter to Krupskaya, he gave a more detailed explanation to his assessment of "the will":

> Dear Nadezhda Konstantinovna!
>
> I dare bother you only owing to the great importance of the issue in question. What I mean is Vladimir Ilyich's so-called "will." It's needless to say that, from my viewpoint, the issue of Vladimir Ilyich's well-known letter is perfectly clear in its political and Party aspects, i.e., such an "issue" is nonexistent. However, some belated repercussions may, as such, turn into a political issue.[35]

Mentioning further that Eastman was speaking about "the will," Trotsky noted that, "Only a fool or criminal might have tried to turn Vladimir Ilyich's letter into an instrument of struggle." And since there were both fools and criminals in the world, it would be a good thing to stop them by publishing a statement. And he offered the text of a supposed denunciation, to be signed by Lenin's sister, Mariya Ulyanova, and Politburo members, which he "delicately" suggested that Krupskaya publish.[36]

Trotsky advised Krupskaya to stress the idea that "Vladimir Ilyich had left no 'will' at all," since "the whiteguard press usually refers to 'the will' (in a totally distorted form), having in mind one of Lenin's letters that presents advice of an organizational nature. The Thirteenth Party Congress," he went on, "thoroughly studied that letter, just like all others, and drew from it relevant conclusions in accordance with the circumstances and conditions of the situation. All talk

---

35. Ibid., sh. 63.
36. Ibid., sh. 62.

Lenin, 1922.

Lenin and Stalin in Gorky, 1922.

Stalin, Rykov, Kamenev, and Zinoviev, early 1920s.

Trotsky, 1918.

Bukharin in 1920.

about a concealed . . . 'will' is malicious deception and is directed entirely against Vladimir Ilyich's actual will and the interests of the Party founded by him."[37]

This was not a draft statement, Trotsky stressed in conclusion, but just a statement of a few basic ideas. In reality, however, this was a finished draft, and was later used by Krupskaya. Trotsky assured Krupskaya that he had not yet submitted any proposal to anyone. "You are the first to whom I am writing about [the matter]. Of course, you will decide for yourself in what way and manner you will express your attitude to this proposal."[38]

In reality, Trotsky had written a statement, "About Eastman's Book, *After Lenin's Death*,"[39] back on June 25, in which he said, in particular: "In his book, Eastman mentions several times that the CC 'has concealed' a number of exceptionally important documents, written by Lenin in the last period of his life (such as letters on the national problem, the so-called will, etc.)." He went on to say that those letters, contrary to Eastman's view, were not planned for publication and had indeed been read to the delegates of the Twelfth and Thirteenth Party Congresses.[40]

Further Trotsky stated categorically, "Vladimir Ilyich has not left any 'will'," for the very "nature of his attitude to the Party, just as the Party's nature, ruled out the possibility of such a 'will'."[41] He explained that the letter referred to as "the will" by the foreign press (bourgeois and

---

37. Ibid., sh. 63.
38. Ibid.
39. "Po povodu knigi Istmena 'Posle smerti Lenina'."
40. RCPSMHD, f. 325, op. 1, d. 417, sh. 92.
41. Ibid.

Menshevik) was in reality one of Lenin's "letters with advice of an organizational nature."

Trotsky also described as "erroneous" Eastman's "allegations that the CC had planned not to publish Lenin's article on the Workers' and Peasants' Inspection"; and he quoted the following excerpt from an informational CC letter to Local Party Committees dated January 27, 1923:

> Without discussing any possible historical dangers in that purely informational letter, the issue raised by Comrade Lenin in his article [on the Workers' and Peasants' Inspection] was quite topical, so in order to avoid any misunderstanding, members of the Politburo and the Orgburo deem it necessary to make a unanimous statement that in the CC internal work there are no circumstances that might give any grounds for taking steps to prevent a split.[42]

It was not by accident that Trotsky quoted this lengthy extract from a letter of 1923. His intention was to stress the key role he then played in the Party, and that "the document has not only my signature (among ten others), but the very text was written by me."

Trotsky drew attention to a number of Eastman's factual errors in the book and refused to admit that he was on friendly terms with the book's author. This is what he wrote on that score:

> By taking a clue from Eastman and by citing his views, the bourgeois press—and especially the Menshevik press—emphasizes in every possible way our "close" friendship,

---

42. Ibid., sh. 93.

since he has written a book devoted to my life story, in
an attempt to add, in a roundabout way, more weight to
his conclusions—a weight that they do not and cannot
have.[43]

The main issue was that, by saying all that Trotsky
sought to conceal, it was he who had informed Eastman
about the details of the intra-party discussion. "It seems to
me, however," he wrote, "that a serious and thoughtful reader
has no need to check Eastman's references and his 'documents'—and that, incidentally, not everybody is in a position
to do so."

At the end of his statement of June 25, 1925, Trotsky
wrote, "His book may be of use exclusively to the inveterate
enemies of communism and the revolution. And this is the
gist of its political meaning and its verdict."[44]

However, Trotsky's "soft" assessment of Eastman's book
did not suit Stalin at all. Having read Trotsky's statement,
Bukharin, Zinovyev, Rykov, and Stalin sent a letter to
Trotsky, couched in very sharp terms. This letter has been
lost, but Trotsky's reply to it, dated June 27, 1925, has been
preserved. It follows from this reply that the authors of the
collective letter demanded that Trotsky use such words as
"slander" and "counterrevolutionary" in his statement on
Eastman's book. Trotsky, who did not think that this was
essential, replied, "The main task of the meeting [at which
the guidelines for Trotsky's statement were discussed] was,
I believe, to agree how the most topical and important issue
of the so-called 'will' should be formulated."[45] It is clear that

43. Ibid., sh. 94.
44. Ibid., sh. 96.
45. Ibid., sh. 137–138.

Stalin's group and Trotsky had quite different goals. The General Secretary and his associates set themselves the task of making short work of Eastman (and thereby of Trotsky), and Trotsky wished to prove in any possible way that Lenin's document existed.

Stalin and his group could not care less about Trotsky's attempts at explaining "how a person [Eastman], who viewed the revolution and the Party with respect and understanding, could have taken a hostile stand toward the Party and the revolution, under the influence of factors of minor importance." Stalin's group, according to Trotsky, insisted that "Eastman should be disqualified, not by way of explanation of his evolution, but by means of a sharp political assessment." As a result, Trotsky accepted that principle and, as he believed, "produced a sharper political assessment." In his reply of June 27, 1925, Trotsky made a concession. "I agree," he wrote, "that in his work, Eastman . . . describes our Party leadership in terms that can only be described as slanderous."

In their collective letter, Stalin's group demanded that Trotsky remove from his letter the passage about Rykov's appointment as chairman of the Council of People's Commissars, as well as the passage about the role Trotsky played in writing the letter to the Local Party Committees in January 1923. Since Trotsky had nominated Rykov to that post, he attempted to justify himself:

> In reply to the Politburo's request, I sent a cable from Tiflis and nominated Comrade Rykov for that post, which can be proved by documents kept in the CC archives. So why should I not mention it? I cannot see the point. Similarly, Comrade Stalin suggests I not mention that it was I who

wrote the CC letter to the Local Party Committees, which explained that there was nothing in the work of the CC that might give grounds to speak of the possibility of a split.[46]

Ultimately, Trotsky managed to prove his point to a certain extent: he deleted the passage concerning his role in Rykov's appointment, but did mention that he was the author of the letter to the Local Party Committees. Shortly afterwards, on July 29, 1925, Trotsky wrote another explanation, whose handwritten original has been preserved. It was marked "Top Secret. To the Inquiry of the CC of the French Communist Party about the Journal of Monatte and Rosmer," referring to the journal, *Proletarian Revolution*, which was published in France, and which advertised Eastman's book widely.[47] Trotsky pointed out that he had been acquainted with both Monatte and Rosmer since 1915:

> Rosmer was among the founders of the Third International. Monatte had long resisted joining the French Communist Party, saying that it is headed by many elements interested mainly in making a career of being in parliament. After the Fourth Comintern Congress when, with the help of the French left wing, led by Rosmer, our French Party purged reformists from its ranks, Monatte joined it.[48]

Noting further that he had not played an active role in the affairs of the French Communist Party since the winter of 1923/1924, Trotsky stated:

---

46. Ibid.
47. Ibid., sh. 150–152.
48. Ibid., sh. 150.

> The French Party was then being rent by inner struggles,
> the roots of which were connected with the repercussions
> of the Russian Discussion—struggles that led to the
> expulsion of Rosmer and Monatte from the French Party.

Trotsky pointed out that if he had taken part in those events, he would have "no doubt resolutely" opposed that. Nonetheless, since these events had taken place, Monatte and Rosmer had to act "as the Party's soldiers" and seek "their restoration into its ranks sooner or later." However, having founded their journal, they were too much preoccupied with the defense of what they believed was the correct stance. As a result, the journal became "a weapon aimed against the proletarian revolution, which has been incarnated in the Soviet Union and the Russian Communist Party."[49]

Trotsky also pointed out that the journal (which devoted "a certain space" to Trotsky's apology) offered an interpretation of his views "that has nothing in common with reality." Finally, having expressed the hope that Monatte and Rosmer would put an end to their criticism of the Russian Communist Party, Trotsky gave the following advice to them: "close down the journal immediately; while staying outside the Party, act as the soldiers of the Party, [and] apply to the Comintern Executive with a request to review your case."[50]

Thus, by late June 1925, Trotsky dissociated himself from

---

49. Ibid.

50. Ibid., sh. 152. [Editor's note: ". . . while staying outside the Party, act as the soldiers of the Party. . . ." In others words, so as not to give the impression that their personal actions are sanctioned by the Party, they should temporarily resign. Though this would leave them free to act to the Party's benefit, the Party would not be implicated in any of their actions.]

his followers—not only from Eastman, but also from those who upheld Eastman's views in France. (It was Rosmer who had advised Eastman to publish his book.)

After Trotsky had agreed to make the changes in his statement, Stalin left Moscow to spend his leave in Sochi. During this time his functions were performed by Molotov in Moscow in order to complete the operation against Trotsky that had begun so successfully. However, soon afterwards the plans of Stalin's group were thwarted. On July 16, 1925, *L'humanité* carried the initial version of Trotsky's statement without the changes that Stalin had insisted upon. The article had been handed over to the newspaper's editorial office by D. Manuilsky, member of the Comintern Executive. The article was accompanied by a special resolution endorsed by the FCP CC, in which Eastman's book was described as "a vulgar counterrevolutionary product, a collection of gossip," written "with the express purpose of compromising the Soviet leadership." The FCP CC also expressed its surprise regarding Trotsky's statement, saying that "Comrade Trotsky's reply to that dirty book is too delicate, not categorical enough, almost ambiguous." And due to its ambiguity, the FCP CC believed, Trotsky's reply was even more dangerous than Eastman's book itself. It was also stated that the CC had not received from Trotsky any reply to the demand that he sever contacts with the people from the *Proletarian Revolution* (i.e., Suvarin, Rosmer, and Monatte), thereby making it possible for them "to continue making use of his name even today in order to fight against the FCP." In conclusion, the FCP CC demanded that Trotsky discard his ambiguous stance "in between the Comintern and the worst enemies of communism" and give a clear-cut reply.

The resulting situation irritated practically everybody. Stalin had his doubts on having learned that Manuilsky had handed over the initial version of Trotsky's draft article to *L'humanité* by mistake. In his letter to Molotov dated August 1, 1925, he wrote:

> I was told that Manuilsky had handed over Trotsky's initial draft article on purpose, not by mistake. If that is true, it's a disgrace. If that is true, then we are faced not with "a mistake," as you are writing me, but with a policy pursued by some persons who, for some reason, have no stake in the publication of the final version of Trotsky's article. There is no doubt about it. We must not leave it at that. I suggest that the matter be discussed at a meeting of the seven[51] and that Manuilsky be condemned for his unacceptable action, by which the RCP and *L'humanité* have landed in an awkward position. And we must by all means find out who it was who had compelled Manuilsky to act in such a dirty way. Here are some facts for you to ponder over: a) the documents were handed over to Manuilsky at his written request (which should be kept in the CC archives) with the knowledge of the seven (the issue of handing the documents over to Manuilsky was raised by Zinovyev for the seven to decide); b) the documents were issued when we did not as yet have the final version of Trotsky's article; c) they were issued for the purpose of being studied by the Comintern Executive, not for publication.[52]

---

51. The "seven" consisted of six Politburo members and Kuibyshev, the president of the CCC. Max Eastman deals with this group in his *New York Times* article. See pages 193-194.

52. *Izvestiya CPSU CC*, 1990, no. 9, p. 188.

Stalin further reminded Molotov that at the meeting of the seven it had been decided to publish Stalin's memo of June 18, 1925, to the Politburo on the Eastman affair only after the publication of Trotsky's statement. That is why Stalin objected to the publication of Trotsky's article without Stalin's memo and the other accompanying documents that would throw light on the allegation that "Trotsky had written the article only under CC pressure." "Otherwise," Stalin noted, "Trotsky might look like the Party's savior." Those words show why Stalin had objected to Trotsky's mentioning the decision-making role he had played in the key issues of the country's development. Moreover, Stalin could see through Trotsky's maneuvers, for Trotsky wished to make the most even out of this most unfavorable situation.

In another letter (written after August 1, 1925), Stalin again reminded the seven that it was necessary to publish Trotsky's paper and Krupskaya's letter "in the Russian press" (after publication abroad), for their publication would be of considerable importance, especially now that Manuilsky had managed to muddle things up and thereby willy-nilly raise the issue of the authenticity of Trotsky's article."[53] Indeed, readers in the West could then not make head or tail of the contradictory situation around Lenin's will. They probably knew that Trotsky was also indignant (which was true) at the publication of the initial version of his article. That is why it was rumored in the communist circles that the article had been cooked up.

On August 9, after receiving another letter from Molotov with the assertion that Manuilsky had acted in agreement with Stalin, Stalin stated this:

---

53. Ibid., p. 189.

I repeat that 1) I handed the documents to Manuilsky in accordance with the decision by the seven for the top Comintern Executive leadership *to study, not for publication.* . . . 3) I gave *no instructions for publication* of the initial version of Trotsky's article—and I could not have done so—to Manuilsky, for I believed, and still believe, that Trotsky's article should be published in its best, not worst, version.

Stalin added that he, Bukharin, Rykov, and Zinovyev had been instructed by the seven "to look through" Krupskaya's article prior to its publication. That publication, Stalin stressed, should not have been accompanied by a discussion. Stalin regarded Manuilsky's action as "a dirty business" and a thieving practice that was probably part of the intrigue directed against him personally.[54]

In the final analysis, Stalin attained his goal. The September 1925 issue of the *Bolshevik* journal carried, among its other articles, Lev Trotsky's "About Eastman's Book, *After Lenin's Death*," and Nadezhda Krupskaya's, "To the Editorial Office of the *Sunday Worker*."[55]

Trotsky's statement was a model product of the Party falsification kitchen, a mixture of fact and fiction, which, on the one hand, reflected the eventual triumph of Stalin and his attitude toward and assessment of Lenin's will. In his statement, Trotsky was obliged to keep to Stalin's guidelines, which were outlined in the June 18 memo to the meeting of the Politburo. So Trotsky retracted the assessment he had given from January through October 1923 in a number

---

54. Ibid., pp. 190–191.
55. *Bolshevik*, 1925, no. 16, pp. 67–73.

of his letters to the CC and in his addresses to the Party Plenums.

On the surface, Trotsky's initial stand, explaining the gist of the matter, looked objective. He asserted that Lenin "had left no 'will' at all," and that the very "nature of his attitude to the Party, just as the Party's nature, ruled out the possibility of such a 'will'."[56] It should be stressed that this assertion was true—up to a point. It was true only at the time that Lenin was dictating his letters; but after Lenin's death those documents automatically became his political will. Meanwhile, under Stalin's pressure, Trotsky tried to convince the Party that Lenin's letters were addressed exclusively "to the guiding bodies of the Party and its Congress." They included, Trotsky continued, "advice of an organizational nature," and had not been concealed from the Party, since the Thirteenth Party Congress received them "with the greatest attention" and drew "conclusions in accordance with the circumstances and conditions of the situation."[57]

At the same time, Trotsky refuted his own statements. Thus he wrote that, contrary to Eastman's allegations, the CC did not intend to "hush up" Lenin's article on the Workers' and Peasants' Inspection. Moreover, in order to prove it, Trotsky cited an excerpt from the classified letter to Local Party Committees dated January 27, 1923, and in the new situation he distorted the real facts. It should be recalled that in January 1923 Trotsky quite correctly believed that Stalin's entire Secretariat had no intention of publishing Lenin's article. It should also be recalled that Trotsky's stand on that matter was well known to the European communist

---

56. Ibid., p. 68.
57. Ibid.

parties from his letter to the CC, written back in 1923 and published (in a translation close to the original) in the *Sotzialisticheskií Vestnik* (*Socialist Bulletin*).

Naturally, Western European communists had food for thought in this respect. Krupskaya's stand on the matter was far from simple. Back in the autumn of 1923, after the October CC Plenum, she made it clear to the troika, in her letter to Zinovyev, that it was an open secret to her that Stalin was familiar with the contents of the "Letter to the Congress."[58] As noted above, when she handed over Lenin's documents in May 1924, Krupskaya intimated that she wished to publish Lenin's notes of December 24-25, 1922 and January 4, 1923. Later, at the Plenum, held in July 1926, as we shall see, she was even more insistent upon pursuing her aim. However, in 1925 Krupskaya, found herself isolated on this matter, for none of the Politburo members supported her. At that time even Lenin's sister, Mariya Ilyinichna Ulyanova, did not share her view.

In her 1925 statement, Krupskaya, just like Trotsky, isolated the "Letter to the Congress" from the other works written by Lenin in late 1922 through early 1923, and asserted that "the letters to the Congress are not a 'will'." At the same time, Krupskaya was the first to state the following to the Soviet press: "Lenin's will, in the real sense of the word, is immeasurably broader—it is expressed in V.I.'s last articles." And Krupskaya stressed that all of them had been published.[59] Krupskaya was also the first to broach the subject of the contents of the "Letter to the Congress." Having

---

58. *Izvestiya CPSU CC*, 1989, no. 2, pp. 201-202.

59. Later Nikolaí Bukharin repeated this idea in his article, "Politicheskoe zaveshchanie Lenina" ("Lenin's Political Will") (1929).

made a concession to Stalin by repeating Trotsky's statement that the "Letter to the Congress" had been written for the Party Congress, Krupskaya also stressed Trotsky's responsibility for seeing to it that this letter was read.

The decisive battle between Stalin and his group, on the one hand, and the united opposition, now led by Trotsky, Zinovyev, and Kamenev, on the other, around Lenin's "Letter to the Congress," took place at the Joint Plenum of the Central Committee and the Central Control Commission, held in July 1926. Both sides were using the issue of the publication of Lenin's document as a weapon in settling the basic issues around which an ideological struggle was being waged within the Party. As before, both sides circumvented the main ideas of Lenin's political will, artificially isolating the "Letter to the Congress" from all other works by Lenin. Let us analyze that process.

Seven

The July 1926 Joint Plenum of the Central Committee and the Central Control Commission of the VKP(b)

The Plenum of July 14–23, 1926 played a special role in hushing up Lenin's will. The information about Lenin's final letters was not among the subjects discussed at the first session of this meeting, which was instead devoted to important issues of the country's economic development. However, at the close of the meeting the issue of Lenin's will was mentioned and produced a general tension.

Zinovyev was the first to throw down the gauntlet to Stalin when he addressed the evening session on July 21. He admitted that he had made quite a few mistakes when he opposed Lenin; but Lenin, he now claimed, believed that Zinovyev "had corrected that mistake." However, Zinovyev went on, those present know nothing about his second mistake which he had failed to correct:

141

In late 1922 or early 1923, Vladimir Ilyich warned [the Party] on three points with respect to Com[rade] Stalin. . . . What was the first warning about? Relieve Com[rade] Stalin of his duties as General Secretary, not only for his rude manners (that's a trifle); but, Vladimir Ilyich said, because I am afraid that by concentrating vast power in his hands, Stalin will not always be able to use it objectively. I'm putting it mildly. . . .

The second warning was made by Com[rade] Lenin in his letter on the national problem, in which he alerted the Party against the political mistakes of Com[rade] Stalin and Sergo Ordzhonikidze. . . . Vladimir Ilyich warned the Party against Stalin's mistakes in the sphere of the national problem; and, as a matter of fact, he predicted the Georgian uprising. . . .

The third warning consists of Vladimir Ilyich's personal letter to Com[rade] Stalin in early 1923, in which he severed comradely relations with him. Those three warnings were sufficient [for us] to understand in what a serious and business-like manner Vladimir Ilyich warned the Party against C[omrade] Stalin. Lenin has been proved right on that issue as well.

I believe it was a gross mistake on my part not to have grasped the connection among those three warnings, for I had thought that matters would not be carried so far as they have been through Stalin's efforts.[1]

Then Zinovyev read to the Plenum the letter that he and Bukharin had written to Stalin on August 10, 1923, concerning the will.

---

1. RCPSMHD, f. 17, op. 2, d. 246 (IV), sh. 31.

Yes, there is a letter from V.I. in which he advised [the Twelfth Congress] not to elect you Secretary. We (Bukh[arin], Kamen[ev], and I) decided not to inform you about it for the time being, for an understandable reason: you were taking differences of opinion with V.I. too much to heart as it was, so we did not wish to disturb you.[2]

So, by having mentioned these two documents by Lenin, Zinovyev left it to Stalin to explain his stand not only on the substance of Lenin's criticism expressed in the will, but also on why Lenin's note, in which he threatened to sever relations with Stalin and demanded that the General Secretary beg his wife's pardon, was never read to the Plenum. Stalin managed to find a way out of the situation, which I shall describe below. As to the second document, the General Secretary did not stop at outright deception at the Plenum. He restricted himself to submitting a statement "on a personal matter" dated July 13, 1926:

As to Comrade Zinovyev's personal outbursts in his speech and statement, I declare that . . . I have never received any letter from Bukharin and Zinovyev dated 10 August 1923 in Kislovodsk—a fictitious quotation from a fictitious letter, a figment of the imagination, gossip.

As the reader will soon see, this "figment of the imagination" and "gossip" was discovered and published over 70 years later.[3]

Bukharin proved even more ingenious in the art of deception; he told part of the truth:

---

2. Ibid., sh. 32.
3. Ibid., sh. 105.

As to the "letter dated 10 Aug. 1923," I definitely deny that such a letter was sent. Kamenev was not even present in Kislovodsk at that time. We (Zin[ovye]v and I) sent a letter (via C[omrade] Ordzhonikidze) which was of an entirely different nature. At my request, Stalin returned that letter to me, so I shall read it. (C[omrade] Stalin keeps the original.)

And he then read to the Plenum the letter dated July 29, 1923.

In spite of the heated discussion at the Plenum regarding the struggles of Stalin's faction against "a new opposition," the issue of Lenin's will was constantly being brought up. However, everybody was waiting for Stalin's reply, and he accepted the gauntlet thrown down to him by the opposition on the issue of the will.

Stalin started by describing what had happened at the Plenum. It turned out that "three days ago at a meeting of the CC Politburo," during an interval between the meetings of the Plenum, "Comrade Kamenev accused me of concealing from the Party Lenin's letters, the so-called will." Then Kamenev and Zinovyev "started shouting from their seats that the CC allegedly had concealed Lenin's letters from the Party. . . . Today," Stalin went on to say, "Comrade Trotsky has repeated this here. That . . . is a grave accusation." So he suggested that the Plenum settle the issue in the following way:

Either the accusation is correct, in which case the CC should not stay at the helm even a moment longer; or the CC is not guilty, and has not concealed any documents, in which case Kamenev, Zinovyev, and Trotsky are slandering the CC.[4]

---

4. Ibid., sh. 62.

Stalin resorted to the tried and true tactic used previously in the course of the campaign of "exposing" Eastman with the help of Trotsky. Stalin justly pointed out that "the issue was nothing new." Nevertheless, he described in detail at the Plenum how "a certain counterrevolutionary, Mr. Eastman by name, in his book, *After Lenin's Death*, accused our Party's leadership, our CC, of allegedly concealing Lenin's documents from the Party. He was brazen enough to refer to Comrade Trotsky, and Comrade Trotsky was obliged to dissociate himself from him openly and resolutely in the press." Further, Stalin explained his role in that matter and quoted his memo to the Politburo dated June 18, 1925. He described the further course of events as follows: The Politburo—attended by Trotsky, Kamenev, and Zinovyev—unanimously decided that Trotsky make a statement to the press. Stalin also cited Krupskaya's and Trotsky's addresses, laying special stress on the following words:

> All talk about a concealed or unfulfilled "will" is malicious deception and is directed entirely against Vladimir Ilyich's actual will and the interests of the Party founded by him. (See Comrade Trotsky's article, "About Eastman's Book, *After Lenin's Death*," *Bolshevik*, no. 16, 1 September 1925, p. 68).

By mentioning this similar idea from Trotsky's article (whose co-author was actually Stalin), Stalin hinted unequivocally that the responsibility for Trotsky's article should be borne by all Politburo members:

It would be not amiss to say that Comrade Trotsky's article was received with satisfaction, including by Comrades Kamenev and Zinovyev.[5]

Having given a sound thrashing to Trotsky, Kamenev, and Zinovyev, Stalin also remembered Krupskaya's address. He cited a lengthy quotation from her article, where she stated in particular that Eastman was openly slandering the CC by proclaiming that Lenin's will had allegedly been concealed.

"Such, Comrades, are the facts," Stalin declared. ". . . They testify that Lenin's will with respect to his letters has been fulfilled by the CC completely and thoroughly." Then Stalin addressed a question/accusation to Trotsky, Zinovyev, and Krupskaya: Why, contrary to facts, "are they now repeating Eastman's slanderous statements? And am I not right in asserting that they are slandering the Party?" Indeed, what could all those people reply at that time, after their year-old statements had been reread, without putting themselves in an embarrassing situation, of which Stalin was now taking advantage?

In his address, Stalin also raised the issue of the publication of Lenin's letters. "I am holding in my hands three of Lenin's letters: First, a letter with character descriptions; second, on the national problem; third, Comrade Lenin's letter about Comrades Kamenev and Zinovyev dated October 1923. None of them has yet been either printed or published." Pointing out that the first two letters had been read at the Twelfth and Thirteenth Party Congresses, Stalin stressed that the letter about Kamenev and Zinovyev "had not been

---

5. Ibid., sh. 62–63.

read at any of the Congresses, and that none of the CCC members knows anything about it."[6]

The General Secretary stressed stubbornly that he had always insisted not only on "reading" but also on publishing the will, but that he had not been permitted to do so. "I inform all of you," Stalin said, "that not a single hand, including those of Zinovyev and Kamenev, was raised at the Thirteenth Congress to vote for publishing those letters— the Congress unanimously, Trotsky included, voted against publishing those letters." Stalin assured the Congress that, just as before, he believed those documents should be published, for "the Joint Plenum of the CC and the CCC has every right to have those letters read here" and be later "added to the minutes."[7]

However, the course of events was altered by Krupskaya's and Kamenev's addresses. Having finally comprehended, at least to a certain extent, the situation at hand, Krupskaya tried to convince the audience that Lenin's wish was to have the contents of the will brought to the notice of all the Party. She said this, in particular:

Ilyich wished that [the will] become known to the Party. He did not specify in what form that should be done, for his condition was very grave. But he instructed me to do all that was necessary for the Party to learn the contents of that document. Since the first article had an inscription, "To the Party Congress," I found it necessary to apply to the Central Committee, so that the Central Committee could find suitable methods of informing the Party about the

---

6. Ibid., sh. 64.
7. Ibid.

articles that are called the "will." To read them at the Congress—that decision was adopted by the Politburo, the leadership, who decided in what form the Party should be informed.[8]

Krupskaya was perfectly right in this respect, but Rykov, who chaired the meeting, immediately attempted to disprove her statement.

I am holding the authentic document, written by Nadezhda Krupskaya. She has just stated that prior to the Thirteenth Party Congress she insisted *on informing the Party* of the contents of Comrade Lenin's document, which is often described as the "will," *which naturally implies a broader majority than the Party Congress.* I shall read out what she wrote on May 18, 1924—the document has been signed by her, "N. Krupskaya."

". . . Vladimir Ilyich expressed his firm desire that after his death *the next Party Congress should be informed* of the contents of this transcript. N. Krupskaya."[9]

Now you've heard Nadezhda Krupskaya's statement which runs counter to what she wrote herself in her letter on May 18, 1924. . . .

I'm saying this because allegations are being made here that someone is concealing documents, after all those comrades themselves have signed what I have just read and what was eventually done, i.e., the documents, mentioned in the above-quoted note were made known to the Thirteenth Party Congress. That's why Comrade Trotsky was right in describing in the press as a slanderous statement

---

8. Ibid.
9. Ibid., sh. 65.

against the Party that those documents had been concealed by somebody from someone." [Italics added.][10]

It should be pointed out that Rykov was running a great risk by reading Krupskaya's document, for he read only a part of it to the audience. He omitted the note that Krupskaya had written on that same sheet of paper on May 18, 1924, in which she maintained that Lenin's documents were meant "for the Party." That was clearly foul play. After this, Rykov raised the issue of reading Lenin's documents. It was unanimously decided to read them at the Plenum and include them in the record of proceedings. Then Stalin took the floor.

Noting in passing that he did not wish to take part in the bickering which was "taking place among the comrades here," he methodically read Lenin's documents. He started with Lenin's letter with the well known character descriptions (December 24–25, 1922), and "Supplement to the Letter" (January 4, 1923).

This done, Stalin made "a few remarks," whose purpose was to remind the Plenum that exactly the same meeting nominated him to the post of General Secretary in spite of Lenin's objections. True, some of those who had not attended the previous Congresses were among the present audience; so they were now faced with many new facts. It should be noted that Stalin asserted, seemingly quite logically, that Lenin had offered "to think over" the issue of his replacement as General Secretary, and "all delegations without exception," he reminded his audience, had come on record for "Stalin acting as General Secretary in the future as well." Further, he reminded everyone that even "at the next meeting"

---

10. Ibid.

held after that Congress, he submitted his resignation, which was not accepted. "What could I do after that, Comrades?" Stalin exclaimed. "I cannot act independently, so I obeyed the Plenum's decision." After the story of Stalin's "compulsory" appointment as General Secretary had been fed to the Plenum, Stalin briefly informed the meeting that he would do his best "to mend his rude manners, to reform."[11]

It transpired somehow that Stalin even protected Trotsky, when in the course of the discussion, held in 1923–1924, "a section of our Party demanded that strong measures be adopted with respect to Trotsky," but Stalin objected to "Trotsky's dismissal from the post of a Politburo member," and claimed that at that time he "held a moderate, not openly inimical, stand against Trotsky."

As soon as Trotsky heard that, he could not help but remark, "No one will believe that," and immediately he heard the answer from the hall, "Ask your associate Zinovyev; he will tell you." That exchange of caustic remarks in the hall had an explanation, about which many of the delegates knew nothing; namely that at this time Stalin indeed objected to "extreme" measures, as proposed by Zinovyev and Kamenev, being taken against Trotsky. Stalin objected for two reasons: first, he took into account Trotsky's authority, well aware that Trotsky enjoyed the support of influential, if not numerous, circles in the Party; and secondly (and mainly), because he regarded Trotsky as a counterweight to Zinovyev and Kamenev.

At the Plenum, however, Stalin cleverly disguised his real attitude toward his sworn enemy Trotsky. By mixing fact and fiction, Stalin tried to win over to his side the

---

11. Ibid., sh. 66.

uninitiated who did not know the intricacies of the past political struggles for power within the CC.

"I am speaking to the Joint Plenum of the CC and the CCC," was Stalin's reply to Trotsky. "I declare that I had kept to a moderate policy with respect to Trotsky. I said that Trotsky should continue discharging his duties in the Politburo; and I, together with the majority of the CC, won the case."[12]

Noting further that it was Trotsky's own decision whether or not to believe him, Stalin again took up the subject of the will, and drew the following conclusion from what was said there: ". . . I was trying to take into account Lenin's instructions with respect to Trotsky, and I was doing my best to pacify Comrades Kamenev and Zinovyev, who demanded Comrade Trotsky's expulsion from the Party."

Stalin's attempt at the Plenum to "defend" Trotsky against his former enemies who had now become his allies, did not prevent him from reminding those present, with reference to the will, of Trotsky's political sins. "The letter says," Stalin went on in his attempt to give his own interpretation to the will, "that Trotsky 'was not to blame personally' for his 'non-Bolshevism'; so it follows that Comrade Trotsky should drop his 'self-assurance' and 'non-Bolshevist views'."

According to Stalin's logic, Trotsky had not changed his stand, had not acted on Lenin's advice. "But it does not . . . at all follow from all this," the General Secretary went on, "that Comrade Trotsky has thereby been granted the right to revise Leninism and that we should accept Trotsky's revision of Leninism. No one has said here that Comrade

---

12. Ibid.

Trotsky is not to blame for his non-Bolshevism.'"

In response to that obviously illiterate pronouncement, Trotsky remarked, with reference to "non-Bolshevism", "Former." Stalin's then made a maneuver to produce an impression on the audience, none of whom had ever seen the will, and many of whom had learned for the first time about its contents at this meeting. His reply to Trotsky was: "The word 'former' is not mentioned in the letter; it says only 'non-Bolshevism'; so if he is not to blame for non-Bolshevism, he is free, he believes, to revise Leninism."[13]

Stalin's interpretation of the views Trotsky held in the distant and not-so-distant past met with support from the audience. Having read Lenin's letter on the national problem, Stalin, at Trotsky's request, read the other two documents: Lenin's letter to Trotsky, dated March 5, 1923, with a request "to undertake a defense of the Georgian case"; and the note dated March 6, 1923, addressed to "Comrades Mdivani, Makharadze, and others" on the same issue. And then Stalin either made an attempt at checking to what extent Trotsky remembered the situation in March 1923, or perhaps he simply made a mistake while reading the note. In either case, Stalin concluded Lenin's note to Trotsky dated March 5 with the following words: "With communist greetings, Lenin."

Trotsky then remarked, "Either the note was copied down inaccurately, or there's another note there; for I remember very well that there must be a note which was signed 'with best comradely greetings,' not 'with communist greetings'." The audience responded to this adequately, but some of the delegates made such remarks as "such pettiness; probably you'd like to change Lenin's words?" "Self-assurance." Stalin

---

13. Ibid.

was quick to rise to the situation: "Yes, the note says, 'with best comradely greetings'." It should be noted that the concluding words in this note were exactly as Trotsky remembered them. Indeed, all documents from that period in 1923 were kept by Trotsky's secretariat in a file, which has been preserved.[14]

All of the above most likely took place because there was probably one more note from Lenin to Trotsky, and because Stalin wished to find out whether or not Trotsky knew anything about it. It turned out that Trotsky did not, so Stalin did not worry any longer; and so he left yet another piece of evidence about his far from "dogmatic" attitude toward Lenin's texts.

Stalin spared no effort at the meeting to prove that there was no fundamental difference between his opinion and Lenin's. "You can see," Stalin went on, after having read the note dated March 6, 1923, "that in this letter, just as in his previous one, Lenin did not utter a word about fundamental contradictions—he is speaking exclusively about Stalin's connivance at Ordzhonikidze's actions, about 'persecutions' in connection with 'the Georgian case.' A special commission has studied that issue, and the comrades know to what extent Comrade Mdivani is right or wrong."[15] In discussing this issue in passing, Stalin neglected to stress that his stand on the national problem did not contradict Lenin's accusations, and so he started to read "Letter to Bolshevik Party Members," written back in October 1917, and indicated that Kamenev and Zinovyev had joined forces in opposing Lenin.

---

14. Ibid., sh. 69.
15. Ibid.

Stalin's calculation was simple: having learned about it, even those who had been vacillating would draw the conclusion pronounced by Voroshilov; namely, "Then everything was exactly the way it is now. That hits the nail on the head." Stalin did not merely read the document; he added: "I believe that any comment to this letter would be superfluous."

However, that was not the end of the matter. After his criticism of Kamenev and Zinovyev, Stalin again took up the subject of Trotsky. He contended that, had Lenin written his will not in 1922 but later, after a discussion was held in the Party about Trotsky, he would have assessed Trotsky's political profile differently.

> I may refer to a number of documents that testify that, in various periods and various circumstances, Lenin expressed various views of Comrade Trotsky. In '22, when he wrote his "will," prior to the '23 discussion, prior to the decision adopted by the Fifth Congress of the Comintern in '24, when there was as yet no open revisionism of Leninism, Lenin wrote one thing. . . . Who will dare assert that Lenin would have written the same about Trotsky two years later, in 1924, when Trotsky started openly revising Lenin?[16]

Further the General Secretary quoted an extract from an article written by Trotsky back in 1911. The situation in that period (when Trotsky was bringing together an anti-Leninist bloc) was very similar, Stalin believed, to "the current situation in the Party when an anti-Party bloc is

---

16. Ibid., sh. 71.

in the process of formation," this time spearheaded against Stalin.[17]

The discussion around Lenin's will continued even after Stalin's address. Participants exchanged written statements "on a personal matter," which were placed at the end of the verbatim record of the July 1926 Joint Plenum of the CC and the CCC. Only a few members of the Party elite were informed of them. What were some of these statements?

Grigorií Zinovyev was second among those who made statements. Without mentioning the will, he nevertheless spoke "about Stalin's address." Zinovyev pointed out that the General Secretary sought to join forces with him after the Fourteenth Party Congress in the struggle against Trotsky, on the one hand, and with Trotsky against him, on the other. Zinovyev believed that his own new bloc (with Kamenev and Trotsky) was "based on principle" and that its purpose was to struggle "against deviations from the Leninist line."[18]

In his statement on "a personal matter," Trotsky maintained that Stalin's attempt "to make use of Chkheidze's letter once again" revealed that the General Secretary was "not a totally loyal" person. Trotsky wrote:

> That letter was written at a moment of fierce interfactional struggle. Lenin was one hundred percent correct in that struggle. That struggle has long been a thing of the past. That letter, written 13 years ago, now seems to me entirely incomprehensible, just as it must seem to any other member of our Party. Digging in the dustbin of old interfactional

---

17. Ibid.
18. Ibid., sh. 103.

struggles can only be done for the purpose of stunning young Party members, who know nothing about the past, i.e., exclusively for the sake of scandal and intrigues. . . .[19]

This was precisely the sort of disloyalty Lenin had in mind when he insisted on January 4, 1923 upon dismissing the General Secretary from his post.

Further, Trotsky pointed out:

In his so-called "will," Vladimir Ilyich told me what he considered important to tell—in terms that he found suitable, taking a general view of the past (including the past interfactional struggle) in an effort to help the Party in its future work. In his speech, Comrade Stalin was seeking to decide for Lenin how Lenin might have reacted now, in the context of the present struggle. That was fundamentally wrong, for had Lenin been with us now, Comrade Stalin would not have held the post of General Secretary and would not have been able, by manipulating the Party apparatus, to destroy its political course and disorganize the leading cadres that were formed in Lenin's time. In that case the current struggle would not have been waged.[20]

Trotsky found himself in a quandary. The General Secretary had described him as the vehicle of Eastman's ideas with respect to the assessment of the will. At the same time, Stalin stressed that Trotsky had condemned Eastman. However, Trotsky was not to be outplayed: He found a way out by stating the following:

---

19. Ibid., sh. 103–104.
20. Ibid., sh. 103.

I came out against Eastman after the issue of the will had been turned into something like an international sensation spearheaded against the Party. But this is not to deny that "the will" as such had to be quoted at meetings by heart, because the Party had not been familiarized with its contents as Lenin wrote it. . . . In particular, the passage where Lenin has in mind my post and speaks about my "non-Bolshevism" was intentionally misinterpreted by Comrade Stalin and others as if Lenin described me as non-Bolshevik. Then the question arises: How could Lenin have demanded that a Politburo member, a non-Bolshevik, not be reminded about his non-Bolshevism? In this case by slandering me, Lenin is slandered.[21]

Comrade Bukharin's statement "on a personal matter" was quite lengthy:

In connection with Lenin's "will," which has been read here, I deem it my Party duty to make the following statement.

First, I believe that Comrade Lenin was perfectly right, both substantively and tactically, by having pointed out, in 1922, my theoretical deviations, which, in the final analysis, could be reduced to insufficient comprehension of dialectics. Second, I believe that Comrade Lenin was quite right, for those theoretical mistakes were directly reflected in the erroneous political line that I pursued in the past. All of you remember that my dispute with Lenin about dialectic was bound up with the discussion about trade unions, in which I took Trotsky's side and even extended my hand to the Shlyapnikov group. Third, those

---

21. Ibid., sh. 104.

theoretical errors were reflected politically in my stand, which was close to that of Trotsky (Brest, trade unions); and I did not grasp the significance of the manner in which Lenin raised the issue of peasantry. Fourth, I have taken due account of Comrade Lenin's "will." I hope in the near future to present to the Party, if my political duties permit me [the time], a suitable theoretical work. In political respects, after the trade union discussion, I did away with what remained of my Trotskyite delusions; for Trotskyism is based on bombastic formalism, not on Lenin's creative dialectics.[22]

. . . In view of Comrade Zinovyev's statement about the letter to Stalin, sent from Kislovodsk and dated August 10, 1923, I deem it necessary to state the following:

In Kislovodsk I took part in elaborating the plan of reorganizing the Secretariat and the Orgburo. I personally proceeded from the desire to unite the leading CC members in the top CC leadership, that is, Stalin, Trotsky, and Zinovyev. I believed that the danger of atomization of the leadership was looming large before the Party, and I was doing my best to ensure peace in the Party ranks by coordinating various trends in the leadership. That plan has fallen through. In Kislovodsk, Comrade Zin[ovyev] was vacillating, and soon afterwards he started fiercely attacking Trotsky and disrupted that plan. Comrade Trotsky, for his part, left no stone unturned to dampen relations (the 1923 discussion was held a few months after that letter was sent). Thus, relationships within the Party assumed an entirely different nature. As to the "letter dated 10 Aug. 1923," I definitely deny that such a letter was sent. Kamenev was not even present in Kislovodsk at that time. We (Zin[ovyev] and I) sent a letter (via C[omrade]

---

22. Ibid., sh. 104.

Ordzhonikidze) which was of an entirely different nature. At my request, Stalin returned that letter to me, so I shall read it. (C[omrade] Stalin keeps the original.)[23]

And so he read the letter:

Sun., 29/VII 23.

To Stalin and Kamenev.

Sergo [Ordzhonikidze] will tell you about ideas fostered by two Kislovodsk residents. Naturally we should discuss this matter together many times before adopting any decision. Greetings! Sincerely yours,

G. Zinovyev.

Isn't it beastly of you not to write anything to us?

Grigorií described us as "residents" in his modest way. Greetings! Please inform us: What do you think about our plan?—at least in a few words, but as soon as possible.

N. Bukharin.[24]

Here it should be stressed again that Stalin, who no doubt had read everything that Lenin had dictated, had always consistently denied that he had done so. (It was only in 1991 that, at long last, the correspondence between Bukharin and Stalin was published.) In 1923 Zinovyev and Bukharin spent their leave in Kislovodsk. Stalin and Kamenev stayed in Moscow, and Stalin then began making important decisions on his own. Zinovyev, supported by Bukharin, objected to this. The following letter, among other

---

23. Ibid.
24. Ibid.

things, bespeaks the nature of disaffection that had been manifested:

G.E. Zinovyev to L.B. Kamenev[25]
30 July 1923, Kislovodsk

Dear L.B.,

Let me tell you that this time we are quite seriously and deeply indignant. Indeed! We are staying here not without your permission while you are in Moscow. You wield considerable influence. And you permit Stalin to have such a mocking attitude.

Shall I cite facts? Examples?

You'll have them!

1) *The National Problem.* We've spared no effort to reach political accord on that issue! Even Sergo [Ordzhonikidze] admitted recently that we were quite right. A certain clever reactionary writes this in *Nov[oe] Vr[emya]*[26] (Sofiya): "B[olshevi]ks once again hit the nail on the head; their resol[ution] of the nat[ional] question is of even greater importance than the NEP."

Did Stalin consult anybody when he made those appointments? He certainly did not consult us. And I'm afraid that he did not consult you either. What then do we have as a result? He acts as he pleases. And V.I. spoke about it even at the Tenth Congress: A political line is worth nothing if its implementation is distorted organizationally.

2) *The Convention on the Straits.* Why did no one consult Trotsky or us on this important issue? *There was enough time to do so.* By the way, I have been entrusted

---

25. This letter is written on Presidium of the Comintern Executive letterhead.

26. *New Time*, a newspaper.

with the functions of a consultant of the People's Commissariat for Foreign Affairs. Honestly, would Lenin have ever acted like that, without consulting by cable members of the Politburo? Never! We've discussed this matter here with eight CC members—all of them believe that the signing of the convention was a mistake. The same in Ioffe's case. He's sick, isn't he? His deputy might have been sent there. Would Lenin recall anyone without consulting anyone? Never! Recall, for instance, what was done in the past, say, something like plans to appoint someone like Lomonosov.

3) *The Comintern.* After a ten-minute talk with that intrigue-spinner Radek, Stalin immediately decided that the German CC was incompetent; that Bukh[arin], Tsetk[in], Brandl[er], and I had not gained an insight into the matter; and that that windbag Radek should be supported—who all but "convinced" the fascists with his speech about Schlagetter. In this matter, Stalin proved quite efficient—he sent cables to Trotsky and others.

What is this?!

V.I. spent ten percent of his time on Comintern affairs; each week he discussed them with us for hours, and even though he had information on the international movement at his fingertips, he never acted on the spur of the moment without questioning all of us 20 times. And Stalin acted according to the principle of "I came, I saw, I conquered," probably regarding Bukharin and me as "dead bodies"— he has no need to consult us! Neither did he show you our cable, I guess, for he clearly did not consult you.

We informed him (by cable) that we would attend the meeting of the Politburo, even though we were on leave, if the Politburo wished to discuss this important issue. And he did not even condescend to answer us.

4) *Pravda.* This morning (and this was the last straw,

indeed), Bukharin learned from a private cable[27] sent by Dubrovskii that, without informing and consulting Bukh[arin], steps were taken to make reappointments in the *Pravda* editorial office—Radek and others were among its seven newly appointed members. Was this done out of spite? What would Stalin have said if he were on leave instead and, without informing and consulting him, we had appointed new CC Secretariat or the Board of the People's Commissariat for National Affairs?!

Bukh[arin] has done much more for *Pravda* than Stalin or any of us has. In general, goddammit, I can't see why Stalin should treat such people as Bukh[arin] *in this way.*

Shall I continue? It seems I've told you enough.

We shall not tolerate such things any longer.

If the Party is destined to live through a period (prob[ably] *very* short) of Stalin's arbitrary rule—let it be so. However, I, at least, have no intention of concealing all those swinish tricks. They are talking in all the platforms about "the troika" in the belief that I, too, play not the least role in it. In reality there is no troika, only Stalin's dictatorship. Ilyich was one hundred percent right. Either a serious way out will be found or a period of struggle will inevitably set in. Well, there is nothing new in it for you. You spoke about it quite often. However, I was most surprised that Voroshilov, Frunze, and Sergo are of the same opinion. Please, write me what you think about this. Anyhow, our rest has been spoilt. We shall probably soon leave for Moscow. Your self-possession is an excellent thing, but you carry it to the point of callousness. Yes.

Best greetings. Sincerely yours,
G. Zin[ovyev][28]

---

27. This cable has not been discovered.
28. *Izvestiya CPSU CC*, 1991, no. 4, pp. 197–198.

The subsequent correspondence dealt with the project, put forward by Zinovyev and Bukharin, or reorganizing the work of the CC Secretariat and the Orgburo Administration. However, the essential matter for the present study is that Zinovyev now sent a letter informing Stalin of Lenin's demand that he be removed from the post of General Secretary.

In his letter of reply, Stalin pretended that he knew nothing about it. He wrote:

J.V. Stalin to G.E. Zinovyev
7 August 1923, Moscow
(And for Bukharin)
A copy for Voroshilov

Comrade Zinovyev!

I acknowledge the receipt of your letter dated 31/VII. I answer in accordance with your questions.

1. You write this: "do not interpret the talk with Sergo in a different way."[29] I'll tell you openly that I have interpreted it "in a different way." We are faced with the following alternative: *either* the Secretary should be replaced immediately *or* plans should be made to appoint a special political committee to supervise his activity. Instead of a clear-cut formulation of the question, both of you are beating about the bush in an effort to attain the goal in a roundabout way, probably calculating on the people's stupidity. Why do you need those roundabout ways, if there is really a group and a minimum of trust? *Why did you need references to some letter by Lenin of which I know nothing, regarding the Secretary* [italics

---

29. In his letter of July 31, 1923, Zinovyev actually wrote: "Do not interpret this negatively."

added]. Is there no proof that I do not attach much value to my job and am not afraid of letters? How would you describe a group whose members are out to intimidate one another (to say the least)? I accept the idea of replacing the Secretary, but I object to the establishment of the institution of [another] political committee. (There are many political committees as it is: the Orgburo, the Politburo, the Plenum.)

2. You are wrong when you say that the Secretary settles all issues arbitrarily. *Not a single* decision, *not a single* instruction is endorsed without the respective copies being sent to the CC archives. I wish you would discover at least a single message, a single instruction in the CC archives that has not been sanctioned by some CC body or other.

3. You are wrong when you say that the Politburo agenda is planned by one person. The agenda is written on the basis of all questions received at the Secretariat meetings, with due account of the opinions expressed by *Kamenev* (the Politburo chairman) and *Kuĭbyshev* (the Central Control Commission chairman). It would be even better if all members of the group or of the Politburo wished to be present when the agenda is discussed. Not a single question can be "swept under the rug," not only because that would run counter to the instructions, but also because the above-mentioned persons are a sufficient guarantee against [any question being shelved].

4. The decision on the Straits was adopted unanimously. Chicherin objected to it meekly, while Litvinov resolutely demanded that it should be signed. Not a single Politburo member raised the issue of consulting those who were absent. Trotsky had left a note with a request not to even be sent the record of proceedings of the Politburo. He had not given a definite reply to my question about

the composition of the RVSR.[30] He is probably in need of a really good rest. Before departure not a single word was said by either of you about the need to consult you. Moreover, it is not always possible to consult people by wire due to the great number of documents. As to the substance of the matter, we could not have acted otherwise (we must have inspection in the Straits in order to kick up a row in case of delays in our grain exports, etc.). Even Chicherin has now renounced his former stand.

5. Ioffe was relieved of his duties primarily owing to his wife's request. I enclose the respective documents.[31] (He is *gravely* ill.)

6. The Putilov plant will certainly not be closed down. But we must raise the issue in S[t.] P[etersburg],[32] for the Presidium of the Supreme Council of the National Economy, led by Rykov, insists on it.

7. Zorin was long ago appointed secretary of the Iv[anovo]-Voz[neseviskiĭ] Local Committee.

8. As to Germany, Radek has nothing to do with the issue. Should Communists strive (at the current stage) to seize power without social democrats; are they prepared to do so? That is the question, I believe. When we were taking over in Russia, we had certain resources such as:

---

30. Military Revolutionary Council of the Republic.

31. The documents have not been discovered in the archives.

32. On the basis of a Glavmetall report, on July 30, 1923, the Supreme Council of the National Economy (SCNE) adopted a decision on closing the Putilov plant in view of its supposed unprofitability in 1923–1924. The issue of the Putilov plant was discussed at a Politburo meeting on August 21, 1923, and it was decided to decline the SCNE request to close the plant. [Editor's note: "Glavmetall" literally translates "Heavy Metal." This was a department dealing with metallurgy within the Ministry of Heavy Industry.]

a) peace; b) land to peasants; c) support by the overwhelming majority of the working class; d) a sympathetic attitude on the part of peasants. The German Communists have none of those advantages. Of course, they have the Land of Soviets as their neighbor, which we did not have, but what can we do for them at this juncture? If the present German government tumbles, so to say, and the Communists come to power, nothing will come of it; it would end in a fiasco at best. And if it comes to the worst, they will be vanquished and thrown back where they began. The important thing is that Brandler wishes to "teach the masses." The bourgeoisie, jointly with right-wing social democrats, would have certainly turned that demonstration training into the final battle (so far they have every chance to do so) and would have defeated them. The fascists naturally will not be caught napping, but it would be better for us if the fascists were the first to attack—in that case the entire working class would rally around the communists (Germany is, by far, not Bulgaria). Moreover, all indications are that the fascists' positions are weak in Germany. The Germans, I believe, should be bridled, not encouraged.

With best wishes,

J. Stalin

P.S. I shall go on leave on 15/VIII.

I am sending a copy to Comrade Voroshilov, for Sergo has said that he is keeping abreast of the issue and shows interest in it.

J. St.[33]

Zinovyev and Bukharin wrote in reply:

---

33. *Izvestiya CPSU CC*, 1991, no. 4, pp. 203–204.

G.E. Zinovyev, N.I. Bukharin to J.V. Stalin[34]
10 August 1923, Kislovodsk

Comrade Stalin,

We shall answer point by point.

1) It is clear that you are displeased that we had also contacted, via Sergo, Vorosh[ilov]. a) They are your friends and ours; b) you also discussed those subjects with them more than once; c) the discussion was started in Moscow on many occasions but you were too irritated to continue it. We have long been disaffected, but we purposely decided in Moscow first to have some rest, calm down, and then raise the issue.

2) Lenin's letter. Yes, there is a letter from V.I. in which he advised [the Twelfth Congress] not to elect you Secretary. We (Bukh[arin], Kamen[ev], and I [Zinovyev]) decided not to inform you about it for the time being, for an understandable reason: you were taking differences of opinion with V.I. too much to heart as it was, so we did not wish to disturb you.

3) "There is a group," you write. It exists *badly*. We told you about it on many occasions in Moscow.

4) "The respective copies being sent to the CC archives." That is not the point. It is the substance that matters, not formal aspects.

5) We have learned for the first time that Kamenev and Kuíb[yshev] are taking an active part in preliminary

---

34. This letter was written in Bukharin's hand and signed by Zinovyev. The following words were written in the end by Zinovyev: "To Comrade *K. Voroshilov*. Dear Comrade, I am sending you a copy of our reply to Koba. Kamenev writes that he fully supports our proposal and that 'after scolding,' Koba will also accept it. Come to visit us for a day or two. Greetings! Sincerely yours, G. Zin[ovyev]."

discussions of the Politburo agenda. This practice must be new. At least Kamen[ev] often complained for the same reason we did.

6) The Issue of the Straits. Once more your answer is formal: "not a single word was said by either of you about the need to consult you." Such things are done without any requests; that is, when very important matters are at issue and when "a group" exists.

7) Ioffe. Since he is so gravely ill, he should certainly be relieved of his duties. However, Levin's cable[35] was dated 6 Aug, i.e., after he had been relieved of his duties. It should have been done more tactfully.

8) Germany. I am sure we shall soon have to make historic decisions (in 1 or 2 years at most). But the dispute was not about this. No one was going "to seize power." There was no threat of "the July days." The GCP CC parried brilliantly the fascist threat of shooting down every tenth striker: the communists said that in that case they would shoot down every fifth fascist. Radek described this as a "mistake." Without consulting anyone, he sent a "personal" letter to disavow the GCP CC. We objected. You took Radek's side. Without consulting us, you delayed the dispatch of our cable and sent a cable to Tr[otsky].[36] Such things are not done, even if there was no "group." We informed you that we were prepared to come to Moscow— two w[eeks] ago. Yesterday Kamenev cabled us that he had learned about it for the first time ever.[37]

9) The Pravda editorial office. You did not say a word

---

35. They probably mean L.G. Levin (1870–1938), who, since 1920, had been head of the Occupational Therapy Division of the Kremlin Hospital. His cable has not been discovered.

36. This cable has not been discovered.

37. This cable has not been discovered.

about it to Bukh[arin]. How could you? What would you say, if in your absence, we had set about appointing the Secretariat Collegium, even if it were a temporary appointment?

10) Appointment of CC instructors on the national problem. That was a controversial, delicate issue. You did not consult either us or Kamenev.

11) Stupid quarrels with the S[t.] P[etersburg] Local Party Committee.[38] All the Trotskyites are already talking about them—don't worry. This Committee's bureau (the c[omrade]s who are closest to y[ou]) *all* feel offended.

But all those are petty details.

The essential thing is: Lenin is not here. Therefore the CC Secretariat is *objectively* starting to play the same role in the CC that the Secretariat plays in any Local Party Committee, i.e., *in fact* (<u>not</u> formally) performs *all decision making*. This it is impossible to deny. No one wishes to appoint political committees (you often describe the Org[buro], the Politburo, and the Plenum as political committees!). But the *real* (not fictitious) existence of "the group" and *equitable* cooperation and a responsible attitude are *impossible* under the present regime. That's a fact. Willy-nilly you faced us with *faits accomplis* scores of times. Meanwhile, the situation (with Tr[otsky] as well as with various platforms) is becoming increasingly complicated, and disaffection within the Party is growing (do not look at the surface). Hence the search for a better form of cooperation.

---

38. He must be referring here to the conflict between Stalin and the Secretary of the Petersburg Local Committee and Northwest Bureau of the CC of RCP(b) P.A. Zalutzkiĭ on the attempt to move I.M. Moskvin from Petrograd and appoint him as Vice-Chairman of the Organizational Department of the CC of RCP(b).

It would be *empty talk* to discuss "positions," etc. Neither you nor we need such [positions], of course. It would be *empty talk* to discuss "severing relations." The Party will not let it happen. We do not want it. We shall step aside at best. There is no other core [faction or group]. And it will cope with the situation, *if you wish*. We cannot imagine it without you.

Where shall you spend your leave? Very soon (by the end of the month) we'll come to Tiflis. If you wish, we would be only too happy to visit you and stay for a day.

We have no doubts whatsoever that we shall come to terms. Have a good rest. Best wishes.

G. Zin[ovyev].[39]

So Stalin left documents in which he officially denied that he had read Lenin's note of January 4, 1923. Although Zinovyev was well aware of this, he was powerless to prove that he was right at the July 1926 Plenum.

Mariya Ilyinichna Ulyanova, Lenin's sister, also sent a letter to the Presidium of the 1926 Joint Plenum meeting. She took Stalin's side without any reservations, stating the following, in particular:

V.I. held Stalin in high esteem. Characteristically, in the spring of 1922, when V.I. had his first stroke, and also when he was bedridden after his second stroke in December 1922, V.I. summoned Stalin and made quite an intimate request, which one would address only to a trusted person and one who was regarded as a true revolutionary, as a close friend. And Ilyich stressed at that time that it was Stalin and no one else that he wished to talk to. Generally,

---

39. *Izvestiya CPSU CC*, 1991, no. 4, pp. 205–206.

while he was bedridden, so long as he could communicate with comrades, he summoned Stalin more often than anyone else, and at the hardest moments of his illness, he summoned Stalin exclusively, and no other CC member.[40]

Here Mariya Ulyanova had in view the case when Lenin asked Stalin to fetch him poison.

In her reminiscences, written long after the July 1926 Plenum, she interpreted this statement, which had obviously been written under Stalin's pressure and with Bukharin's "assistance," differently. As a matter of fact, she denounced all she had written for that meeting. This time she wrote that she "had not told the whole truth about V.I.'s attitude to Stalin"[41]:

The aim of the statement, written at the request of Bukharin and Stalin, was to protect him [Stalin] from the opposition's attacks by referring to Ilyich's attitude toward him. The opposition speculated on V.I.'s last letter to Stalin, in which he raised the question of severing relations with Stalin. The immediate reason for this was of a personal nature, for V.I. was indignant at Stalin's having spoken rudely with N[adezhda] K[rupskaya]. That exclusively and primarily personal, as it seemed to me at that time, motive was used by Zinovyev, Kamenev, and others for political purposes—and for factional purposes—but with the passage of time, in comparing that fact with a number of V.I.'s pronouncements, as well as with Stalin's entire behavior after Lenin's death, his "political line," I became increasingly aware of Ilyich's real attitude to Stalin during the last period of his life.[42]

---

40. RCPSMHD, f. 17, op. 2, d. 246 (IV), sh. 104.
41. *Izvestiya CPSU CC*, 1989, no. 12, p. 196.
42. Ibid., pp. 196–197.

After her belated "revelation," Mariya Ilyinichna Ulyanova adduced a great number of facts to explain the change in her view of Lenin's attitude to Stalin. In particular, she stressed Lenin's self-possession and pointed out that although he had no warm feelings for Trotsky, he nevertheless valued his abilities highly. She wrote:

> It was extremely difficult to maintain a balance between Trotsky and other Politburo members, especially between Trotsky and Stalin. Both of them were extremely ambitious and intolerant. They put personal motives before business interests. . . . V.I.'s authority was a restraining factor for them; and so their mutual hostility did not then reach the stage it did after V.I.'s death.[43]

She also explained the nature of the "personal" commissions Stalin received from Lenin:

> In the winters of 20–21 and 21–22, V.I. felt unwell; headaches and the loss of the ability to work disturbed him very much. I do not remember precisely when, but once, in that period, V.I. told Stalin that he would most likely eventually become paralyzed; so he made Stalin promise to help him to obtain potassium cyanide. St[alin] promised. Why did V.I. address that request to St[alin]? Because he knew him as a firm, strong-willed person who was never moved by any sentimental considerations. There was no one else he could have asked to do it.[44]

Ulyanova writes that:

---

43. Ibid., p. 197.
44. Ibid.

V.I. addressed the same request to Stalin in May 1922, after his first stroke. V.I. decided then that it was all over for him and demanded that St[alin] pay him a visit for a few moments. His request was so insistent that they could not refuse him. Indeed, St[alin] then spent some five minutes, no more, at V.I.'s bedside. On leaving I[lyi]ch's room, he told Bukharin and me that V.I. had asked him for poison, for, he said, it was time to keep his promise. So Stalin promised to do so. They kissed each other and St[alin] left. But later, having discussed all this together, we decided that V.I. should be reassured, and Stalin returned to V.I. and said that after he had consulted the doctors, he believed that there was yet some hope and the time had not yet come to keep his promise. V.I. livened up visibly and agreed, although he said this to Stalin: "Cunning, aren't you?" "Can you say that I was ever cunning?" Stalin replied. They parted and did not see each other until V.I. felt better. . . .[45]

These statements from Ulyanova are convincing evidence in favor of the opinion that Stalin had poisoned Lenin—which Trotsky had written about not long before his death.

Now let us return to the discussion of the July 1926 Plenum. In her statement, Ulyanova touched on another most important problem:

An incident took place during Stalin's visit to Lenin, which was mentioned by Zinovyev in his address—it happened not long before the loss of Ilyich's capacity of speech (March 1923)—but it was of a strictly personal nature and had nothing to do with politics. Comrade Zinovyev knows this

---

45. Ibid., p. 198.

full well and there was no need to refer to it. That incident took place because Stalin had reprimanded Lenin's family for having violated the doctors' instructions that, during the period of aggravation of Lenin's disease, they should not inform him of political news, in order not to disturb him and aggravate his condition. Ilyich, who had learned about this by accident—and such protective regimens had always irritated him—reprimanded Stalin, in his turn. Comrade Stalin begged his pardon, and that was the end of it. Naturally, if Ilyich, as I have mentioned, had not been in a very grave condition, he would have reacted differently to that incident. Documents about the incident are at my disposal, so I may produce that at once, if the CC wishes to examine them.

So I assert that all talk by the opposition about V.I.'s attitude to Stalin absolutely does not correspond to the reality. Those relations have been and are the most close and comradely.

M. Ulyanova

26 July 1926.[46]

Many years later, however, she explained that incident in a different way:

Stalin phoned her and began to explain to her rather sharply, apparently believing that V.I. would not learn about this conversation, that she should not talk business with V.I. . . . .

You know what happened next—we have already covered this in chapter three. On one occasion Stalin sum-

---

46. RCPSMHD, f. 17, op. 2, d. 246 (IV), sh. 104.

moned Ulyanova to his office and started complaining that he could hardly sleep at night because Lenin had a grudge against him. He asked her to intercede for him with Lenin, which she did, but Lenin did not respond to that maneuver.[47]

Stalin left to posterity a detailed and clear-cut statement of his views. Here are some of the eight points of his statement at the Plenum of the Executive Committee. In one of them, he refers to Trotsky as a slanderer. Characteristically, Stalin started by making Trotsky call Eastman a slanderer and ended by declaring that Trotsky himself was a slanderer.

1. Comrade Trotsky is wrong in saying that Lenin "insisted" on relieving Stalin of "his duties of General Secretary." In reality, Lenin "suggested" that the Party Congress "think over" the matter of Stalin's reappointment, and he left the matter for the Party to decide. And having thought it over, the Congress decided unanimously that Stalin should go on performing the duties of General Secretary, so Stalin could not but obey that decision.

2. Comrade Trotsky is wrong in asserting that if Stalin did not hold the post of Secretary, "there would be no struggle now." Stalin did not hold the post of Secretary either in 1920 or in 1918; however, Trotsky was engaged in fierce struggle in the course of him campaign against the Party and Lenin both in 1918 (the Brest Peace) and 1920 (the trade union discussion). Does Trotsky believe that the alliance he formed in August with Potresov and Alexinskií is attributable to Stalin's "disloyalty"? The struggle Lenin had carried on for three years against Trotsky's August bloc was characteristically explained by Trotsky at that time not so much by considerations of

47. *Izvestiya CPSU CC*, 1989, no. 12, p. 198.

principle as by "low squabbles fanned up by Lenin, who is a past master in things like that" (see Trotsky's letter to Chkheidze). It is high time to understand that it is stupid to attribute differences of opinion in the Party to "personal factors". . . .

5. Comrade Trotsky was wrong in asserting that Lenin "offered not to bring up his [Trotsky's] non-Bolshevism." In reality, Lenin asserted in his "will" that "Trotsky is hardly to be blamed for his non-Bolshevism personally." Those are quite different things. Trotsky's "non-Bolshevism" is a fact. That Trotsky is hardly "to be blamed personally" for non-Bolshevism is also a fact. But that Trotsky's non-Bolshevism is real and that it is necessary to fight against it is also a fact, and there is no doubt about it. Lenin should not be distorted.

6. Comrade Trotsky cannot deny that Eastman's slander about our Party's efforts "to hush up" Lenin's documents was stamped with ignominy by Trotsky himself; and that later, forgetting all about it, Trotsky thus found himself among those who are slandering our Party. No statement can alter that fact.

7. As to Trotsky's letter to Chkheidze, Trotsky must know that I am not obliged to conceal Trotsky's sins and pass over in silence Party documents. Trotsky's letter to Chkheidze is a very important Party document which already belongs to our Party's history. The history of our Party and of our contradictions is not a "dustbin," as Trotsky puts it. All our young people study our Party's history, which is a part of their education. So historical documents should not be passed over in silence.

8. As to Comrade Zinovyev's personal outbursts in his speech and statement, I declare that: a) I have never received any letter from Bukharin and Zinovyev dated 10 August 1923 in Kislovodsk—a fictitious quotation from

a fictitious letter, a figment of the imagination, gossip; b) Lenin had never "severed" personal comradely relations with me—that is a slanderous allegation by a person who has lost his head. One may judge Lenin's personal attitude to me at least by his entrusting me, during the period of his illness, on several occasions with such important tasks that he never even tried to entrust either to Zinovyev or Kamenev or Trotsky. Politburo members and Comrades Krupskaya and Mariya Ulyanova know about those tasks; c) neither is it worthwhile to reply to Comrade Zinovyev's allegations about Stalin's "intrigues": One has only to recall Comrade Zinovyev's recent maneuvers; first, when he demanded the isolation of Trotsky and the "worker" opposition; and later, when he struck an alliance with Comrades Trotsky and Medvedev, in order to decide who should be accused of lack of principles and intrigue-spinning and who is engaged in the principled struggle for Leninism.

J. Stalin.

13.VIII.26[48]

---

48. RCPSMHD, f. 17, op. 2, d. 246 (IV), sh. 105.

Eight

The Opposition Struggles

After the July Plenum Lenin's documents became the epi-center of a struggle between the opposition and the CC, backed by the Central Control Commission. Stalin was widely supported in this conflict by the OGPU.[1] The op-position, in its turn, used prerevolutionary methods of under-ground struggle, such as widely distributing among the Party members various secret leaflets and booklets, whose content was often quite extensive.

Let us analyze one of these documents. It is printed on rice paper and was found among the papers stolen from Trotsky in Paris. This untitled document is completely devoted to Lenin's will, which the opposition considered one of its main weapons in the struggle against Stalin. The opposition believed that "the best Leninists were those who helped distribute it."

According to the opposition, the enemies of the will were

---

1. Central United Political Directorate, precursor of the KGB.

Stalinists who kept it hidden away. The Stalinists not only classified the will as secret, but did nothing to implement its ideas. The will was understood to consist not only of Lenin's dictations of December 24-25, 1922 and January 4, 1923, but also of all his "deathbed" articles from late December 1922 through March 1923. Such a broad interpretation of what constituted the will contradicted Stalin's statement made at the July 1926 Plenum, in which he implied that the will was merely the one letter with the character descriptions of Central Committee members.

The opposition considered all of Lenin's dictations to consist primarily of advice on avoiding a possible split in the Party. Stalin, the opposition believed, thought that the split was possible only under Lenin; and that under the current circumstances, he and his faction considered such a split impossible. Indeed, at the July 1926 Plenum, Tomskii confidently said: "Any split is out of the question because there is nobody to split with." And after Stalin's remark, "Quite right," he added, "Take care not to allow a situation in which, instead of a split in the Party, we shall have to cut somebody off."[2] As further events showed, this was not an idle threat. Using the text of the will, the opposition conducted a kind of breakdown of the positive and negative aspects of Stalin, Trotsky, Zinovyev, Kamenev, Bukharin, and Pyatakov. Stalin's character description occupied the central place here. The "negative" aspects of the General Secretary were:

1. Having become General Secretary, Stalin has unlimited authority concentrated in his hands.

---

2. RCPSMHD, f. 17, op. 2, d. 246(IV), sh. 42.

2. I am not sure whether he will always be capable of using that authority with sufficient caution.
3. Stalin is too rude.
4. Not tolerant.
5. Not loyal.
6. Not polite.
7. Not considerate to his comrades.
8. Capricious

Not even Lenin's "etc.," which ended the list of Stalin's "defects," was overlooked during the analysis of negative characteristics. In particular, this document read:

9. "Etc." It is difficult to say what Lenin's word "etc." implied. In any case, this could not have referred to positive qualities.
10. I think relations between them [Stalin and Trotsky] make up the greater part of the danger of a split.[3]

On the other hand, the analysis of Trotsky's positive and negative aspects were:

Negative	Positive
1. He has displayed excessive self-assurance.	1. He is distinguished not only by outstanding ability.
2. Excessive preoccupation with the purely administrative side of the work.	2. He is personally perhaps the most capable man in the present CC.

---

3. RCPSMHD, f. 325, op. 1, d. 417, sh. 75.

3. Perhaps we blame Trotsky too little for his non-Bolshevism.

3. These are the two qualities of the two outstanding leaders [Trotsky and Stalin] of the present CC.

4. The relations between them [Stalin and Trotsky], in my opinion, represent the major threat of the split.

4. Perhaps we blame Trotsky too little for his non-Bolshevism.

On the basis of this breakdown, the reader can conclude that Stalin, though being an "outstanding" leader like Trotsky, had ten negative features of character, while Trotsky had four positive ones and only four negative ones. Trotsky's non-Bolshevism was considered both a "positive" and "negative" aspect of his political profile. This apparently insufficient classification was drawn with one goal in mind: to emphasize the negative appraisal that Lenin gave Stalin, and thereby to demonstrate the "complexity" and "exceptionality" of Trotsky's character.

This document reflects the opposition's understanding of the ways to overcome the split in the Party. The opposition convincingly argued that had the Party followed Lenin's advice in a timely manner, no struggles within the Party would have arisen later.

Basing their work on all the documents Lenin dictated from the end of December 1922 through the spring of 1923, the opposition compiled a program of measures by which Lenin had planned to prevent a split brought about by the conflict between Stalin and Trotsky. These measures were:

1. To increase the number of members of the Central Committee to fifty or one hundred people.
2. To think about a way of removing Comrade Stalin from his post [of General Secretary].
3. To appoint another person in his stead who in all other respects differs from Comrade Stalin in having only one advantage, namely, that of being more tolerant, more loyal, more polite and more considerate to the comrades, less capricious, etc.[4]

Further, the opposition claimed that the threat of a split could be eliminated only if the Plenum of the Central Committee and the Workers' and Peasants' Inspection were reorganized. But the main idea of the opposition's document was more ambitious yet: since the Party did not take into account Lenin's advice, and, moreover, supported Stalin over Trotsky, the opposition concluded that only a collective leadership could replace Lenin.

"All of Lenin's will," the document reads, "is directed against the theory of the 'individual leader' that Comrade Stalin and his faction so diligently propagandize to the Party." Further, it is stated that Lenin did not wish to promote any of the "six" he described [Stalin, Trotsky, Zinovyev, Kamenev, Bukharin, or Pyatakov] to the post of General Secretary.

"COLLECTIVE leadership," the opposition emphasized, "is what Lenin sought when he wrote his will." According to the opposition, Lenin recommended that conditions be established in the headquarters of the Party, in the CC, such that: "(1) negative features of the Party leaders would be

---

4. Ibid., sh. 78.

neutralized; (2) political and theoretical doubts and errors of individual Party leaders would be rendered harmless; (3) the work of a 'strictly centralized and highly authoritative group' (the CC) would be placed under conditions commensurate with its authority; and lastly (4) to establish conditions in which the members of the Central Control Commission would constitute an integrated group, which, 'without regard to individuals,' would see to it that nobody's authority could prevent the making of inquiries or the checking of documents; and which, on the whole, would achieve unconditional possession of information and the most accurate performance. . . ." The main idea of the opposition's document is that Lenin did not conceive the collective leadership with "the General Secretary of the Central Committee in the person of Stalin."[5]

Lenin's will remained "a voice crying in the wilderness": it was classified as secret, unknown to the Party. The Central Committee is solely to blame for the Twelfth, Thirteenth, and Fourteenth Congresses having "bypassed Lenin's will." The authors of this document claimed that the danger posed by allowing Stalin to remain as General Secretary was thoroughly confirmed, and that the prospects of the will's realization were grim.

The opposition rejected the interpretation of the will set forth by Stalin at the July 1926 Joint Plenum. The opposition claimed that Stalin "roughly and disloyally" misinterpreted the will; and believed that, in his speech at the July 1926 Joint Plenum, he did not attach due importance to Lenin's letters by merely saying that, generally speaking, it was wrong to call these letters a "will." The opposition used an interesting

---

5. Ibid., sh. 80.

method of comparing the text of Lenin's will with its interpretation by Stalin in his speech at the July 1926 Joint Plenum[6]:

Original words of Lenin	*Misinterpretation by Comrade Stalin*
1. Stalin is too rude, and this defect, although quite tolerable in our midst and in dealings among us Communists, becomes intolerable in a General Secretary.	
2. That is why I suggest that the comrades think about A WAY OF REMOVING Stalin from that post (i.e., from the post of General Secretary of the CC).	2. Lenin suggested that the Party Congress *think over the question* of Stalin's removal from the post of General Secretary.
3. And *appointing* another man in his stead who in all other respects differs from Comrade Stalin namely in having *only one advantage:* is more tolerant, more loyal, more polite, more considerate to the comrades, less capricious, etc.[7]	3. . . . *and replace* with another person possessing the same qualities etc., *but without* rudeness.

---

6. Ibid., sh. 81.
7. Ibid., sh. 84.

It is one thing to think about "a way of removing," and quite another thing to think over "the question of removal." Yet in his personal declaration at the July 1926 Joint Plenum, Stalin emphasized that Lenin did not "insist" (as Trotsky noted) on his removal from the post of General Secretary, but suggested only "to think over" the question of his removal. How could the Congress "think it over," the opposition reasonably asked, if the delegates at the Thirteenth Congress did not have the text of the will? It should be mentioned that neither was this text available to the participants of the July 1926 Joint Plenum.

In conclusion, the opposition disclosed the plan that they thought had been outlined by Stalin at the July 1926 Joint Plenum: to prepare the publication of Lenin's will within a year; and to contrive to have the Fifteenth Congress, after "having thought over Lenin's will, unanimously vote to keep Stalin as Secretary." As the opposition noted on the eve of the Congress, the necessary steps were taken in this respect:

> Comrade Stalin has already prepared to split the Party by 3/4. Under his influence, Kamenev, Trotsky, and Zinovyev were removed from the CC Politburo, i.e., from the top Party posts. It was not long ago that he tried to exclude them from the CC. The circle of persons Lenin described in his will as being quite eminent and outstanding leaders of our Party, was replaced by Comrade Stalin with his "own" people. Having destroyed and sacked Lenin's Politburo with the help of the "unlimited authority" he has concentrated in his hands and which he uses very carelessly, Stalin is preparing the destruction of Lenin's CC.

Stalin's goal was the following:

(a) *To replace Lenin with Stalin* (he has been working on this for two years). (b) *To dissolve Lenin's Politburo and replace it with Stalin's.* (Lenin's Politburo, which included Lenin, Zinovyev, Trotsky, Kamenev, and Stalin, has already been dismissed, while 4/5 of Stalin's Politburo has already been formed.) (c) *[To effect] Staff changes in Lenin's Central Committee and create Stalin's* Central Committee (this work was started at the Fourteenth Congress, then continued with the expulsion of Lashevich and the attempt to expel Comrades Zinovyev and Trotsky from the CC). (d) *[To make] Changes in Lenin's Party membership,* (to be achieved by "cutting off" and "dropping out," and by overloading the Party with petite bourgeoisie). Taking all this into consideration, this is exactly what Lenin meant by *a split in the Party.*

This is the essence of the "complete elimination of Lenin's will."[8]

It is worth noting that Bukharin and Pyatakov were also given negative descriptions in the opposition's document. Bukharin's characteristics differed from those of Pyatakov (who supported the opposition in 1927).

As for Comrade Bukharin: at the July (1926) Plenum of the Central Committee he said, "I believe that Comrade Lenin was perfectly right, both substantively and tactically(!), by having pointed out, in 1922, my theoretical deviations, which, in the final analysis, could be reduced to insufficient comprehension of dialectics. . . . I have taken due account of Comrade Lenin's "will." I hope in the near future to present to the Party, if my political duties permit me [the time], a suitable theoretical work."[9]

---

8. Ibid., sh. 87.
9. Ibid., sh. 82.

In the opposition's opinion,

Comrade Bukharin's statement has many reservations.
How did Comrade Bukharin come to know that it was
for "tactical" reasons that Lenin pointed out that Comrade
Bukharin's "theoretical views can be classified as fully
Marxist only with great reserve," that "there is something
scholastic in him," and so on? Certainly, Lenin *assumed*
the possibility that Comrade Bukharin *"will find an occasion to enhance his knowledge and amend his one-sidedness."* One and a half years ago, Comrade Bukharin promised to "present to the Party, if his political duties permit
him [the time], a suitable theoretical work." However, the
Party still does not have Comrade Bukharin's "theoretical
work." On the contrary, we now have yet another development of the negative qualities about which Comrade
Lenin spoke. Bukharin's statement does not contain a word
of his attitude toward Lenin's will as a whole, whether
he stands for its implementation, whether he will he
struggle for it, etc. He uttered not a word about it. Is not
the reason for Comrade Bukharin's silence that he once
again trails behind Comrade Stalin and the Stalinists?"[10]

So, we have a document typical of the opposition's interpretation of Lenin's will. Its principle task was to prove that
Trotsky's supporters were true Leninists, while the main
antagonists of the ideas set forth in the will were Stalin
and his faction. It was the General Secretary, the opposition
affirmed, who, having made the will secret, triggered the
split. In its turn, the Central Committee made a blunder in
not having followed Lenin's advice by removing Stalin from

---

10. Ibid., sh. 82–83.

the post of General Secretary. The result of all this was a crisis in the Party that contributed to the split and strengthened Stalin's position as an "impostor" Lenin.

Of course, I do not think that the problem of the Party "split" and the ousting of Stalin's opposition can be reduced only to implementation of the will. The reasons for the split and the ousting were much deeper. The acuteness of the struggle within the Party evidently did not depend on the fulfillment or nonfulfillment of Lenin's advice; it depended on other factors connected with the general social and economic situation in the country, which was being forced in different ways to begin the unpromising construction of state socialism. However, the present study is not concerned with analyzing these factors and their influence on the character of the inner-Party struggle. Analysis of the document quoted above shows not only that the opposition was quite right in describing Stalin's role in hushing up the will, but also that the concealment of Lenin's documents from the Party was a common fault of those who were the main subjects of the will.

Nine

Eastman's Triumph

On October 18, 1926, the *New York Times* published Lenin's dictation of December 24–25, 1922. This document was quoted in full in an article by Max Eastman, in which he again defended Trotsky.[1]

The publication of the will was Eastman's real triumph. It was as if he said, "Look, I was accused of the unforgivable sin—slander and fiction. Now read for yourself; here is the original text of Lenin's record, which was not invented by me, as has been alleged." This was not just another move in the game of political struggle; Eastman made a real breakthrough in information. It was an entire year after the publication of Eastman's article before the Fifteenth Party Congress, at Stalin's initiative, allowed publication of the will along with the dictation of January 4, 1923, in an edition of 13,500 copies (as a Supplement to Secret Bulletin No. 30 of the Fifteenth Congress). Yet even then the documents

---

1. *New York Times*, October 18, 1926, pp. 1 and 5.

were read only by top Party officials, while the Party's lower echelons, as before, remained unaware of them. It was only in 1956 that all of Lenin's dictations from 1922 through 1923 on this problem were published in the *Bolshevik* journal, and later in the 45th volume of V.I. Lenin's *Complete Works*.

In his long article, Max Eastman became the first foreign investigator to substantively comment on Lenin's will. He was not just a commentator, but the man who had earlier written a book expounding the contents of the will. Naturally, he remembered the articles by Trotsky and Krupskaya, who in 1925 had called him a slanderer and a traitor of the ideals of Communism. Remembering that, and understanding the special role Stalin played in this, Eastman directed his main blow against the General Secretary. Writing about the will, Eastman noted that "this document" is only a portion of Lenin's "memorandums" addressed to the Party. Eastman stated that the memo reproached Stalin and Dzerzhinskií for their "administrative impulsiveness" as well as for conducting "a regular Great Russia nationalistic campaign." Pretending that his own attitude toward Trotsky had not changed despite the publication of Trotsky's denunciation of him, Eastman, against all odds, kept defending Trotsky as before. He wrote that in one of his letters, Lenin "conceded that Trotsky was right, and he himself wrong " in the well known polemics on the important question "government planning" [i.e., on the State Planning Commission]. Eastman accepted Trotsky's idea that the will was Lenin's attack on Stalin's enormous power, as well as the recognition of Trotsky's loyalty. He wrote that it was Trotsky whom Lenin trusted and looked upon as his successor. As before, he kept defending all of Trotsky's subsequent struggles against Stalin:

When Trotsky attacked the "triumvirate" [Stalin, Kamenev, Zinovyev] in the Autumn of 1924, demanding that Lenin's fundamental program of "Workers' Democracy" be carried out, he found the whole power of the press and the party machinery and the machinery of the Third International in the hands of his opponents. He was denounced as a counter-revolutionist from one end of the world to the other, his life history was distorted, his writings were falsified and his political position was represented to be exactly opposite to what it was.[2]

It is important to emphasize that what was said about Trotsky (relating to the assessment of his activities of 1924), actually related to Eastman himself. In 1925 Eastman was also blamed for entertaining a counterrevolutionary viewpoint, "the history of his life and activity" was "distorted" and the contents of his work were falsified. Having casually mentioned that his book, *Since Lenin Died*, had been heaped with abuse in fourteen languages by zealous adherents of Zinovyev, Eastman cited the text of the "declaration" signed by Kamenev, Zinovyev, Krupskaya, Trotsky, and Pyatakov. This statement had been deleted from the shorthand report of the July 1926 Joint Plenum. In particular, it read:

Throughout the two years preceding the Fourteenth Party Congress [this period includes the attack upon Trotsky and the events following—M. E.] there existed a fractional "Seven," composed of six members of the Politburo and the President of the Central Control Commission, Kuibesheff. That fractional group, in secrecy from the party, decided in advance every question standing on the order

---

2. Ibid., p. 5, col. 2.

of the day of the Politburo and the Central Committee, and independently decided a series of questions not even considered by the Politburo. It distributed forces in a fractional manner and bound its members within a fractional discipline. In the work of "Seven" there took part, along with Comrade Kuibesheff, those very leaders of the Central Control Commission, Yaroslavsky, Yansen and others, who are conducting a merciless campaign against fractionism. In the ruling group there exists a minority which places fractional discipline higher than the discipline of the party. The task of this whole fractional machine consists in preventing the party from introducing in the normal constitutional manner changes in the policy and composition of its official staff. With every day this fractional organization more and more threatens the unity of the party.[3]

Eastman was living in France in 1925 when he read Trotsky's article, which the English communist newspaper *Sunday Worker* had reprinted from *L'humanité*. He became very upset and suffered from Trotsky's accusing him of slander. Later he wrote, in his book, *Love and Revolution*:

I read in a glance or two the main sentences of Trotsky's disavowal of my book, and of me, my friendship with him, my "Portrait of His Youth"—he made a clean sweep of everything. I groped toward a chair and sank into it, so pale that Eliena thought I was going to faint. I did not faint, but I was sick to my heart. Throughout the world I would be known only for this disgrace.[4]

---

3. Ibid.

4. Max Eastman, *Love and Revolution: My Journey through an Epoch* (New York: Random House, 1964), p. 446. This passage is translated into Russian in V.V. Shvetsov, "Lev Trotskiĭ i Maks Istmen: istoriya

It is necessary to say that the opposition members who had been exiled by that time were very much surprised by Trotsky's action. Like Eastman, they did not know all of the circumstances that had led to this article, which had been prepared not only by Trotsky and Krupskaya, but also by the whole Politburo with Stalin at the head. For instance, N.I. Muralov expressed his bewilderment in his letter to Trotsky, who later published abroad his reply in which he explained that he had sacrificed Eastman in the autumn of 1925, since "the leading opposition members" would not allow him to launch an open struggle against Stalin on account of such a private matter as Eastman's book and all that was associated with it. He explained that his declaration concerning the book had been imposed by the Politburo of the CPSU Central Committee and, in fact, had been written by Stalin.

Eastman could not approve of Trotsky's stand, though he understood that Trotsky had himself become a victim of the political struggle. Eastman wrote on this occasion:

> A political leader should not have done what Trotsky did. Even if I had not consulted with Rakovsky and hence borne the political responsibility, as Trotsky thought, he would have done better to face the facts and allow Stalin to expel him from the Party, if the latter could do such a thing.[5]

It is interesting to note that the will was published in the *New York Times* on the initiative of the opposition. In

---

odnoi politicheskoi dryzhby" ("Lev Trotsky and Max Eastman: The Story of One Political Friendship"), *Novaya i noveĭshaya istoriya* (*New and the Newest History*), 1990, no. 6, p. 153.

5. Shvetsov, ibid.

the autumn of 1926 (a year after Trotsky's article was published in the foreign press and in the *Bolshevik*), the united opposition (Trotsky, Zinovyev, Kamenev) resolved to begin an active campaign against Stalin; and they decided to let Lenin's will again play its part. As Eastman noted later, the text of the "Letter to the Congress" was sent by "a reliable messenger" in Paris to Suvarin, who handed it over to Eastman, who published it. (The $1,000 royalty that Eastman paid to Suvarin and his associates came from the French Communist Party).[6]

However, the opposition failed to take advantage of this. Two days before Eastman's article appeared in the *New York Times*, *Pravda* unexpectedly published a declaration in which the leaders of the opposition, including Trotsky, Kamenev, and Zinovyev, gave up "factional methods" of protecting their views. But this declaration was nothing more than words; the struggle continued, demonstrating the opposition's instability. As for Eastman, though he completely cleared his reputation in the eyes of the foreign communists, his example demonstrated all the "purity" of the struggle around Lenin's will.

Another year passed. In September 1927, 13 members of the Central Committee and the Central Control Commission submitted to the Politburo "The Project of the Platform of Bolshevik-Leninists [opposition] to the Fifteenth Congress of the VKP(b).[7] The Party Crisis and Ways of Overcoming It." This detailed document was a comprehensive program of the Left Opposition.

The Plenum of the Central Committee and the Central

---

6. Ibid.

7. All-Russian Communist Party (Bolshevik), same as the RCP(b).

Control Commission, held on October 22–23, 1927, voted to expel Trotsky and Zinovyev from the Central Committee, while keeping them in the Party. The discussion at the Plenum added nothing new to the scheme that was devised in the struggle between Stalin's group and his opponents (who were ever changing and consolidating) over the issue of the appraisals and ideas given in Lenin's will. At the same time, the assessments of the opposite sides became more definite. Now the main opponents were Trotsky and Stalin; the former supported by Zinovyev, and the latter by Kalinin.

In his speech, Trotsky closely connected the reasons behind the destruction of "the leadership of Lenin's Party" and its replacement by Stalin's ruling group, with its methods of violence now firmly established. He said that Stalin's rudeness and disloyalty, about which Lenin wrote, had become a distinguishing characteristic of the ruling group, of the regime established within the Party. Not rejecting the revolutionary role of violence, Trotsky maintained that violence brings positive results only if subordinated to the "correct" class policy.[8]

Trotsky delivered his last speech in an atmosphere of almost complete obstructionism created by Stalin's faction, who constantly interrupted him and flung insults at him. Nevertheless, he continued his speech, at the end of which he came to Lenin's will. Below are some extracts from the shorthand report of the Plenum, which are characteristic of the atmosphere during this speech:

---

8. RCPSMHD, f. 17, op. 2, d. 329, sh. 88–89.

TROTSKY: The rudeness and disloyalty that Lenin wrote about are now not just personal qualities; they have become the attributes of the ruling faction, its politics, its regime. It is not just a matter of style. The main feature of the present course is that we believe in the omnipotence of violence, even with respect to our own Party. (Noise.)

BABUSHKIN: He reads the *Socialist Bulletin*. A petit bourgeois in the proletarian State.

SKRYPNIK: One more article from *Socialist Bulletin*.

VOICES: Menshevik!

TROTSKY: Through the October Revolution, our Party has obtained a powerful structure for compulsion indispensable to proletarian dictatorship. The core of the dictatorship is the Central Committee of our Party. (Noise.) Under Lenin, under Lenin's Central Committee, the organizing apparatus of the Party was guided by revolutionary class policy on an international scale. From the very beginning, Lenin had misgivings about Stalin becoming General Secretary. "This cook will prepare only spicy dishes," Lenin said, being in a close circle during the Tenth Party Congress. One such spicy dish has been served today under the pretext of a report about the military plot. (Noise.)

VOICES: Menshevik, enough!

TROTSKY: But under Lenin's leadership, under the Leninist body of the Politburo, the General Secretariat played an entirely subordinate role. (Noise.) The situation started to change during the time of Lenin's illness. By the selection of people through the Secretariat, the apparatus group of Stalinists acquired a self-contained character, independent of the political line. That's why Lenin, taking into account his departure from his work, gave his last piece of advice: "Dismiss Stalin, who may bring the Party to a split and downfall." (Noise.)

STEPANOV-SKVORTSOV: Old slander!

TALBERG: Hey, you chatterbox, boaster!

VOICES: Shame!

TALBERG: And is your policy correct?

. . . .

VOICE: Martov!

TROTSKY: (incomprehensible due to the noise and exclamations of protest) . . . The Party did not learn about that advice in due time. The selected apparatus concealed it. And now we are facing the consequences. (Noise.) . . .

VOICE: This is from the *Socialist Bulletin.*

VOICES: Down with Trotsky! Stop talking rubbish! Such things can no longer be tolerated!

TROTSKY: That was a glaring mistake. Violence can play a great revolutionary role, but only on one condition: if it is subordinated to the correct class policy. (Noise.) Under specific historical conditions, the violence used by Bolsheviks against the bourgeoisie, against Mensheviks, against socialist-revolutionaries, produced gigantic results. The violence of Kerenskii and Tsereteli against Bolsheviks only facilitated the defeat of the conciliatory regime. Driving away those people who disagree with their course, depriving them of work, and arresting them, the ruling faction acts against its own Party by every available means. (Noise.)

VOICES: Down with him! What a foulness! Menshevik! A traitor! Stop listening to him! He makes a mockery of the Central Committee!

TROTSKY: A Workers' Party member fears to say in his own cell what he thinks; fears to vote according to his conscience. The apparatus dictatorship (noise) frightens the Party, which should be representative of the proletariat dictatorship. Scaring the Party, the ruling faction. . . .

VOICES: Lie! Down with him!

LOMOV: Fanciful talk but no content. (Noise.)[9]

---

9. Ibid., sh. 89.

Sometime later, Stalin answered the opposition. Directing the main blow against Trotsky, he replied to the accusation of the concealment of the will. Stalin said:

STALIN: . . . that the Congress decided unanimously not to publish it, by the way, because Lenin himself didn't want and didn't demand it. The opposition knows it, as well as we do. And still, the opposition dares say that the Central Committee "conceals" the will. The question about the will was on the agenda, if I'm not mistaken, as early as 1924. There exists a certain Eastman, a former American communist, who was then chucked out of the Party. Having rubbed shoulders with the Moscow Trotskyites, having heard some rumors and hearsay about Lenin's will, this gentleman went abroad and published a book under the title of *After Lenin's Death*. In this book he lays it on thick, blackening the Party, the Central Committee, and the Soviet power. The whole book is based on the allegation that the Central Committee of our Party "conceals" Lenin's will. Since Eastman was for some time socializing with Comrade Trotsky, we, the members of the Politburo, in the person of Comrades Rykov, Zinovyev, Kamenev, Bukharin, Stalin, Molotov, suggested that Comrade Trotsky distance himself from Eastman, who, clutching at Trotsky and referring to the opposition, makes Comrade Trotsky responsible for the slander about our Party in connection with the will. In view of the clarity of the issue, Comrade Trotsky did in fact dissociate himself from Eastman by making a proper declaration in the press. It was published in September 1925, in *Bolshevik*, no. 16. Let me read you an extract from Comrade Trotsky's article concerning the question of concealing or not concealing

Lenin's will by the Party and its Central Committee. I quote Comrade Trotsky's article. . . .[10]

The General Secretary read some extracts from Trotsky's article, and absolutely ignored (as did Trotsky, by the way) Eastman's *New York Times* article. Then he continued:

They say that in this "will" Comrade Lenin suggested that the Congress think over the question of replacing Stalin as General Secretary with another comrade. That is quite right. Let us read this part, though it has already been read at the Plenum several times. Here it is:

"Stalin is too rude; and this defect, although quite tolerable in our midst and in dealings among us Communists, becomes intolerable in a General Secretary. That is why I suggest that the comrades think about a way of removing Comrade Stalin from that post and appointing another man in his stead who in all other respects differs from Comrade Stalin in having only one advantage, namely, that of being more tolerant, more loyal, more polite and more considerate to comrades, less capricious, etc."

Indeed, I am rude, Comrades, to those who rudely and perfidiously destroy and split the Party. I have not hidden this and still do not. At the very first meeting of the Plenum of the CC after the Thirteenth Congress, I asked the Plenum of the Central Committee to dismiss me from the post of General Secretary. The Congress discussed this issue. Each delegation discussed this issue; and all the delegations, including Trotsky, Kamenev, Zinovyev, unanimously obliged Stalin to remain at the post. What should I have done? Should I have quit the post? That's not my nature.

---

10. Ibid., sh. 93.

I've never left any post on my own, and I have no right
to do so, as it would be a desertion. As I have already
said before, I am a dependable man; and when the Party
obliges me, I must obey. A year later, I again submitted
a request to the Plenum to resign, and again they obliged
me to remain at my post. What else could I have done?

As for the publication of the "will": the Congress
decided not to publish it, as it was addressed to the
Congress and was not intended for the press.[11]

At the end of his speech, the General Secretary suggested
publishing the will on the basis of the decision of the Fifteenth
Party Congress. Stalin also referred to the recommendations
regarding publication of the will, which were approved by
the July 1926 Joint Plenum of the Central Committee and
VKP(b) Central Control Commission. As mentioned above,
in accordance with the decision of the Congress in December
1927, a limited secret edition of the will was issued.

Publisher's Postscript

*By then Stalin had consolidated his power. Trotsky was
exiled in 1929. In 1938, Kamenev, Zinovyev, and Bukharin
were executed for treason. Stalin was the absolute master
and ruler of the entire Soviet Union.*

---

11. Ibid., sh. 94.

Appendix 1

A NOTE FROM THE PUBLISHER—To assist readers who might not be intimately familiar with the political history of the Soviet Union in the early 1920s, we print here a chronology of some of the events that are touched upon in this book.

September 15, 1922: The Central Committee of the Georgian Communist Party, after having discussed Stalin's thesis on the establishment of the USSR, supports Georgia's entry into the Soviet Union in line with Stalin's plans.

September 22, 1922: Stalin informs Lenin about this. Lenin, a firm supporter of national autonomy within the Soviet Union, disagrees with this method of Georgia's entry into the USSR. At a Georgian conference on this issue, Ordzhonikidze, who supports Stalin's ideas, slaps one of Stalin's opponents in the face.

October 1922: The Plenum of the Party Central Committee decides against Stalin's thesis.

October 19, 1922: Georgia asks to be admitted into the USSR, not as part of a Transcaucasian federation, as Stalin would prefer, but separately as a Transcaucasian republic. Okudzhava, the Secretary of the Central Committee of the Georgian Communist Party, is then dismissed by the Transcaucasian Territorial Committee.

December 12, 1922: Dzerzhinskií, who had been sent to Georgia and approved Ordzhonikidze's position, reports all that had happened to Lenin, who becomes outraged at the act of physical violence at a political function.

December 18, 1922: At a Central Committee meeting, Stalin is appointed to ensure that the regimen the doctors have prescribed for Lenin is strictly followed. (For fear of agitating his illness, the doctors had insisted that Lenin not be informed of political events and work as little as possible.)

December 21, 1922: Upon receiving permission from Lenin's doctor, Krupskaya (Lenin's wife) takes down a letter that Lenin wishes to dictate to Trotsky. This letter requests that Trotsky adopt Lenin's position on the problems of the monopoly of foreign trade.

December 21 or 22, 1922: Trotsky telephones Kamenev, saying that Lenin asked him to deliver a report on foreign trade to a faction of the Congress and to prepare the ground for putting this question to the Party Congress. Trotsky asks

Kamenev to inform Stalin of this. Kamenev does so, saying that Trotsky apparently means to strengthen his position.

December 22, 1922: Stalin responds to Kamenev, saying that the matter should not be brought to the faction. Stalin wants to know how Lenin managed to correspond with Trotsky, since his doctor had "utterly forbidden" this.

Stalin telephones Krupskaya and brutally intimidates her for allowing Lenin to dictate his December 21 letter to Trotsky and for informing him of political events.

December 23, 1922: Krupskaya complains about Stalin's treatment of her to Kamenev.

Lenin dictates to his secretary Volodicheva the first portion of his "Letter to the [Twelfth] Congress," in which he deals with reorganizing the State Planning Commission, "meeting, in this respect, the wishes of Comrade Trotsky." This letter is shown to Stalin this same day.

Lenin's secretaries maintain a diary of his activities. In her entry for this day, Volodicheva gives no indication that this dictation is confidential. Since Lenin composed this letter in the style of an appeal to Politburo and Central Committee members, it is quite likely that Volodicheva was correct in later affirming that she had received no indication that this dictation was to be confidential.

December 24, 1922: Trotsky sends a draft of changes he wishes to propose regarding the State Planning Commission. He apparently wants this Commission to be in charge of the state economy. Stalin disagrees with Trotsky's plan, and wants the Council of Labor and Defense to be at the head of the administrative machinery. Feeling that his position is strongly threatened by Trotsky's plan, Stalin decides to alter Lenin's December 23 letter.

Stalin, Kamenev, and Bukharin meet with Lenin's doctors, and rule that Lenin is not to be permitted to read newspapers, is not permitted to spend more than five to ten minutes daily giving dictations, and is not to wait for responses to any of his dictations.

Upon learning of this even stricter regimen arranged for him by Stalin and his cohorts, Lenin dictates the second part of his "Letter to the Congress," and keeps this and all future installments confidential. Lenin now stresses to Volodicheva that the previous day's dictation was also confidential, and asks if such was noted on the transcription.

December 24-29, 1922: Volodicheva types Lenin's December 23 letter, making several alterations. One of these alterations changes "meeting, in this respect, the wishes of Comrade Trotsky" to "meeting, in this respect, the wishes of Comrade Trotsky—to a certain extent and on certain conditions."

December 27, 1922: Lenin dictates a letter in which he says that because "personal matters are at present too closely interwoven with the question of principle," Trotsky should not be chairman of the State Planning Commission.

It was perhaps on this day that Trotsky first saw Lenin's letter of December 23, by which time the alterations had already been made.

December 29, 1922: In the late evening, Lenin's chief secretary, Fotieva, visits her direct chief, Kamenev, and verbally and in a written declaration states that after Lenin's letter of December 23 had already been given to Stalin, it was discovered that Lenin had wanted it to be kept in strict confidence, only to be opened after his death. Fearing for his health, Fotieva reassured him that no one apart from his secretariat knew about it and that his instructions had been carried out. Fotieva requests that all who have become acquainted with the letter give no indication to Lenin that its existence is known.

Kamenev sends Fotieva's declaration to Stalin along with a note that makes clear that Trotsky, Bukharin, Ordzhonikidze, Stalin, and possibly but not likely others, know the contents of Lenin's letter of December 23.

Stalin uses Fotieva's declaration to convince Trotsky that it is impossible to get any additional information about Lenin's dictations.

December 30–31, 1922: Lenin dictates "The Question of Nationalities or 'Autonomization'," which is, in part, an attack upon Stalin's and Ordzhonikidze's blunder with the Georgian incident back in October.

January 23, 1923: Lenin's article, "How We Should Reorganize the Workers' and Peasants' Inspection," is delivered to *Pravda* by Lenin's sister, Ulyanova, and is scheduled to be published the next day.

Bukharin won't allow the article to be published, and reads parts of it to Stalin.

January 24, 1923: Lenin sees that his article has not appeared in *Pravda.*

Lenin asks Fotieva to question Dzerzhinskií or Stalin about the commission's materials in the Georgian case. He also asks his secretariat to investigate all the materials about the matter. As his secretaries' diary indicates, this material is needed for his speech at the upcoming Congress.

January 25, 1923: Lenin's article is published in *Pravda,* but with his explicit attack on Stalin deleted.

May 1923: By this time, Kuíbyshev and Kamenev have learned of the contents of Lenin's dictation of December 24–25, 1922.

May 18, 1923: Kuíbyshev, after thoroughly studying Lenin's letters of December 23 and 24–25, 1922, turns them over to the archives, which were then under Kamenev's control.

June 2, 1923: Krupskaya gives Lenin's dictations of the end of December to Zinovyev. A decision is made soon afterwards to send copies of these dictations to Politburo members.

June 8, 1923: Trotsky informs the CC Secretariat that he has not yet received these documents.

Appendix 2

Following are some of the more important dictations by Lenin from December 21 through March 6, 1923. Included are photographic reproductions of the original handwritten text of December 23, 1922 and the official typescript version.

[To Trotsky]

It looks as though it has been possible to take the position without a single shot, by a simple maneuver. I suggest that we should not stop and should continue the offensive, and for that purpose put through a motion to raise at the Party Congress the question of consolidating our foreign trade, and the measures to improve its implementation. This is to be announced in the group of the Congress of Soviets. I hope that you will not object to this, and will not refuse to give a report in the group.

N. Lenin[1]

December 21, 1922

*   *   *

On the following three pages are photographic reproductions of the original handwritten version of Lenin's Letter to the Congress of December 23, 1922 and the official typed text. A translation of this letter appears on pages 15-17. (It is interesting to note that the handwritten text begins with the words "Top Secret," and that the official typed version does not.)

---

1. The signature "N. Lenin" implies that this dictation was taken by Lenin's wife, Nadezhda Krupskaya.

Строго секретно

Письмо к с'езду

Я советовал бы очень предпринять на этом с'езде ряд перемен в нашем политическом строе.

Мне хочется поделиться с Вами теми соображениями, которые я считаю наиболее важными.

В первую голову я ставлю увеличение числа членов Ц. К. до нескольких десятков или даже до сотни. Мне думается, что нашему Центральному Комитету грозили бы большие опасности на случай, если бы течение событий не были бы вполне благоприятны для нас (а на это мы расчитывать не можем), — если бы мы не предприняли такой реформы.

Затем я думаю предложить вниманию с'езда придать законодательный характер на известных условиях решениям Госплана, идя в этом отношении навстречу тов. Троцкому.

Что касается до первого пункта, т. е. до увеличения числа членов Ц. К., то я думаю, что такая вещь нужна и для поднятия авторитета Ц. К. и для серьезной работы по улучшению нашего аппарата, и для предотвращения того, чтобы конфликты небольших частей Ц. К. могли получить слишком непомерное значение для ~~тех~~ всех "судеб" партии.

Мне думается, что 50-100 членов Ц.К. наша партия в праве требовать от рабочего класса и может получить от него из чрезмерного накопления его сил.

Такая реформа значительно увеличила бы прочность нашей партии и облегчила бы для нее борьбу среди враждебных государств, которая, по моему мнению, может и должна ~~взять~~ сильно обостриться в ближайшие годы. Мне думается, что устойчивость нашей партии, благодаря этой мере, выиграла бы в тысячу раз.

Ленин

23/XII —22.

I.-

Письмо к С'езду.

Я советовал бы очень предпринять на этом С'езде ряд перемен в нашем политическом строе.

Мне хочется поделиться с Вами теми соображениями,которые я считаю наиболее важными.

В первую голову я ставлю увеличение числа членов ЦК до нескольких десятков или даже до сотни. Мне думается,что нашему Центральному Комитету грозили бы большие опасности на случай, если бы течение событий не были бы вполне благоприятны для нас /а на это мы разсчитывать не можем/,- если бы мы не предприняли такой реформы.

Затем,я думаю предложить вниманию с'езда придать законодательный характер на известных условиях решениям Госплана,идя в этом отношении навстречу тов.Троцкому,до известной степени и на известных условиях.

Что касается до первого пункта,т.е. до увеличения числа членов Ц.К.,то я думаю,что такая вещь нужна и для поднятия авторитета Ц.К.,и для серьезной работы по улучшению нашего аппарата,и для предотвращения того,чтобы конфликты небольших частей Ц.К. могли получить слишком непомерное значение для всех судеб партии.

Мне думается,что 50-100 членов Ц.К. наша партия вправе требовать от рабочего класса и может получить от него без чрезмерного напряжения его сил.

Такая реформа значительно увеличила бы прочность нашей партии и облегчила бы для нее борьбу среди враждебных государств,которая,по моему мнению,может и должна сильно обостриться в ближайшие годы. Мне думается,что устойчивость нашей партии,благодаря такой мере,выиграла бы в тысячу раз.

Л е н и н .

23.XII.22 г.
Записано М.В.

Continuation of the notes.
December 24, 1922

By stability of the Central Committee, of which I spoke above, I mean measures against a split, as far as such measures can at all be taken. For, of course, the whiteguard in *Russkaya Mysl*[2] (it seems to have been S.S. Oldenburg) was right when, first, in the whiteguards' game against Soviet Russia he banked on a split in our Party; and when, secondly, he banked on grave differences in our Party to cause that split.

Our Party relies on two classes and therefore its instability would be possible and its downfall inevitable if there were no agreement between those two classes. In that event this or that measure, and generally all talk about the stability of our CC, would be futile. No measures of any kind could prevent a split in such a case. But I hope that this is too remote a future and too improbable an event to talk about.

I have in mind stability as a guarantee against a split in the immediate future, and I intend to deal here with a few ideas concerning personal qualities.

I think that from this standpoint the prime factors in the question of stability are such members of the CC as Stalin and Trotsky. I think relations between them make up the greater part of the danger of a split, which could be avoided; and this purpose, in my opinion, would be served, among other things, by increasing the number of CC members to 50 or 100.

Comrade Stalin, having become General Secretary, has unlimited authority concentrated in his hands, and I am not

---

2. *Russian Thought*, a newspaper.

sure whether he will always be capable of using that authority with sufficient caution. Comrade Trotsky, on the other hand, as his struggle against the CC on the question of the People's Commissariat for Communications has already proved, is distinguished not only by outstanding ability. He is personally perhaps the most capable man in the present CC, but he has displayed excessive self-assurance and shown excessive preoccupation with the purely administrative side of the work.

These two qualities of the two outstanding leaders of the present CC can inadvertently lead to a split, and if our Party does not take steps to avert this, the split may come unexpectedly.

I shall not give any further appraisals of the personal qualities of other members of the CC. I shall just recall that the October episode with Zinovyev and Kamenev was, of course, no accident, but neither can the blame for it be laid upon them personally, any more than non-Bolshevism can upon Trotsky.

Speaking of the young CC members, I wish to say a few words about Bukharin and Pyatakov. They are, in my opinion, the most outstanding figures (among the youngest ones), and the following must be borne in mind about them: Bukharin is not only a most valuable and major theorist of the Party; he is also rightly considered the favorite of the whole Party, but his theoretical views can be classified as fully Marxist only with great reserve, for there is something scholastic about him (he has never made a study of dialectics, and, I think, never fully understood it).

December 25. As for Pyatakov, he is unquestionably a man of outstanding will and outstanding ability, but shows too much zeal for administrating and the administrative side of the work to be relied upon in a serious political matter.

Both of these remarks, of course, are made only for the present, on the assumption that both these outstanding and devoted Party workers fail to find an occasion to enhance their knowledge and amend their one-sidedness.

Lenin

December 25, 1922
Taken down by M.V.

*   *   *

ADDITION TO THE LETTER OF DECEMBER 24, 1922

Stalin is too rude, and this defect, although quite tolerable in our midst and in dealings among us Communists, becomes intolerable in a General Secretary. That is why I suggest that the comrades think about a way of removing Stalin from that post and appointing another man in his stead who in all other respects differs from Comrade Stalin in having only one advantage, namely, that of being more tolerant, more loyal, more polite and more considerate to the comrades, less capricious, etc. This circumstance may appear to be a negligible detail. But I think that from the standpoint of safeguards against a split and from the standpoint of what I wrote above about the relationship between Stalin and Trotsky it is not a detail, or it is a detail that can assume decisive importance.

Lenin

Taken down by L.F.
January 4, 1923

*   *   *

Continuation of the notes.

December 26, 1922

The increase in the number of CC members to 50 or even 100 must, in my opinion, serve a double or even a treble purpose: the more members there are in the CC, the more men will be trained in CC work and the less danger there will be of a split due to some indiscretion. The enlistment of many workers to the CC will help the workers to improve our administrative machinery, which is pretty bad. We inherited it, in effect, from the old regime, for it was absolutely impossible to reorganize it in such a short time, especially in conditions of war, famine, etc. That is why those "critics" who point to the defects of our administrative machinery out of mockery or malice may be calmly answered that they do not in the least understand the conditions of the revolution today. It is altogether impossible in five years to reorganize the machinery adequately, especially in the conditions in which our revolution took place. It is enough that in five years we have created a new type of state in which the workers are leading the peasants against the bourgeoisie; and in a hostile international environment this in itself is a gigantic achievement. But knowledge of this must on no account blind us to the fact that, in effect, we took over the old machinery of state from the tsar and the bourgeoisie and that now, with the onset of peace and the satisfaction of the minimum requirements against famine, all our work must be directed toward improving the administrative machinery.

I think that a few dozen workers, being members of the CC, can deal better than anybody else with checking, improving, and remodeling our state apparatus. The Workers' and Peasants' Inspection, on whom this function devolved at the beginning, proved unable to cope with it and can be used only as an "appendage" or, on certain conditions, as an assistant to these members of the CC. In my opinion, the workers admitted to the Central Committee should come preferably not from among those who have had long service in Soviet bodies (in this part of my letter, the term *workers* everywhere includes peasants), because those workers have already acquired the very traditions and the very prejudices that it is desirable to combat.

The working-class members of the CC must be mainly workers of a lower stratum than those promoted in the last five years to work in Soviet bodies; they must be people closer to being rank-and-file workers and peasants, who, however, do not fall into the category of direct or indirect exploiters. I think that by attending all sittings of the CC and all sittings of the Politburo, and by reading all the documents of the CC, such workers can form a staff of devoted supporters of the Soviet system, able, first, to give stability to the CC itself; and second, to work effectively on the renewal and improvement of the state apparatus.

Lenin

Taken down by L.F.
December 26, 1922

*   *   *

Continuation of the notes.
December 27, 1922

GRANTING LEGISLATIVE FUNCTIONS TO
THE STATE PLANNING COMMISSION

This idea was suggested by Comrade Trotsky, it seems, quite a long time ago. I was against it at the time, because I thought that there would then be a fundamental lack of coordination in the system of our legislative institutions. But after closer consideration of the matter, I find that in substance there is a sound idea in it, namely: the State Planning Commission stands somewhat apart from our legislative institutions; although, as a body of experienced people, experts, representatives of science and technology, it is actually in a better position to form a correct judgment of affairs.

However, we have so far proceeded from the principle that the State Planning Commission must provide the state with critically analyzed material and that state institutions must decide state matters. I think that in the present situation, when affairs of state have become unusually complicated, when it is necessary time and again to settle questions of which some require the expert opinion of the members of the State Planning Commission and some do not, and, what is more, to settle matters that need the expert opinion of the State Planning Commission on some points but not on others—I think that we must now take a step toward extending the competence of the State Planning Commission.

I imagine that step to be such that the decisions of the State Planning Commission could not be rejected by ordinary procedure in Soviet bodies, but would need a special procedure to be reconsidered. For example, the question should be submitted to a session of the All-Russia Central Executive Committee, prepared for reconsideration according to a special instruction, involving the drawing up, under special rules, of memoranda to examine whether the State Planning Commission decision is subject to reversal. Lastly, special time limits should be set for the reconsideration of State Planning Commission decisions, etc.

In this respect, I think we can and must accede to the wishes of Comrade Trotsky, but not in the sense that specifically any one of our political leaders, or the Chairman of the Supreme Economic Council, etc., should be Chairman of the State Planning Commission. I think that personal matters are at present too closely interwoven with the question of principle. I think the attacks that are now made against the Chairman of the State Planning Commission, Comrade Krzhizhanovskii, and Comrade Pyatakov, his deputy, and which proceed along two lines, so that, on the one hand, we hear charges of extreme leniency, lack of independent judgment and lack of backbone, and, on the other, charges of excessive coarseness, drill-sergeant methods, lack of solid scientific background, etc.—I think these attacks express two sides of the question, exaggerating them to the extreme, and that in actual fact we need a skillful combination in the State Planning Commission of two types of character, of which one may be exemplified by Comrade Pyatakov and the other by Comrade Krzhizhanovskii.

I think that the State Planning Commission must be headed by a man who, on the one hand, has scientific education, namely, either technical or agronomic, with decades of experience in practical work in the field of technology or of agronomics. I think this man must possess not so much the qualities of an administrator as broad experience and the ability to enlist the services of other men.

Lenin

December 27, 1922
Taken down by M.V.

*   *   *

Continuation of the letter
on the legislative nature of
State Planning Commission decisions.
December 28, 1922

I have noticed that some of our comrades who are able to exercise a decisive influence on the direction of state affairs exaggerate the administrative side, which, of course, is necessary in its time and place, but which should not be confused with the scientific side, with a grasp of the broad facts, the ability to recruit men, etc.

In every state institution, especially in the State Planning Commission, the combination of these two qualities is essential; and when Comrade Krzhizhanovskii told me that he had enlisted the services of Comrade Pyatakov for the Commission and had come to terms with him about the work, I, in consenting to this, on the one hand, entertained certain doubts and, on the other, sometimes hoped that we would thus get the combination of the two types of statesmen. To see whether those hopes are justified, we must now wait and consider the matter on the strength of somewhat longer experience; but in principle, I think, there can be no doubt that such a combination of temperaments and types (of men and qualities) is absolutely necessary for the correct functioning of state institutions. I think that here it is just as harmful to exaggerate "administrating" as it is to exaggerate anything at all. The chief of a state institution must possess a high degree of personal appeal and sufficiently solid scientific and technical knowledge to be able to check people's work. That much is basic. Without it the work cannot be done properly. On the other hand, it is very important that he should be capable of administering and should have a worthy assistant, or assistants, in the matter. The combination of these two qualities in one person will hardly be found, and it is hardly necessary.

Lenin

Taken down by L.F.
December 28, 1922

*   *   *

Continuation of the notes on
the State Planning Commission.
December 29, 1922

The State Planning Commission is apparently developing in all respects into a commission of experts. Such an institution cannot be headed by anybody except a man with great experience and an all-round scientific education in technology. The administrative element must in essence be subsidiary. A certain independence and autonomy of the State Planning Commission is essential for the prestige of this scientific institution and depends on one thing, namely, the conscientiousness of its workers and their conscientious desire to turn our plan of economic and social development into reality.

This last quality may, of course, be found now only as an exception, for the overwhelming majority of scientists, who naturally make up the Commission, are inevitably infected with bourgeois ideas and bourgeois prejudices. The check on them from this standpoint must be the job of several persons who can form the Presidium of the Commission. These must be Communists to keep a day-to-day check on the extent of the bourgeois scientists' devotion to our cause displayed in the whole course of the work and see that they abandon bourgeois prejudices and gradually adopt the socialist standpoint. This work along the twin lines of scientific checking and pure administration should be the ideal of those who run the State Planning Commission in our Republic.

Lenin

Taken down by M.V.
December 29, 1922

*   *   *

Is it rational to divide the work of the State Planning Commission into separate jobs? Should we not, on the contrary, try to build up a group of permanent specialists who would be systematically checked by the Presidium of the Commission and could solve the whole range of problems within its ambit? I think that the latter would be the more reasonable and that we must try to cut down the number of temporary and urgent tasks.

Lenin

December 29, 1922
Taken down by M.V.

*   *   *

Continuation of the notes.
December 29, 1922

(ADDITION TO THE SECTION ON
INCREASING THE NUMBER OF CC MEMBERS)

In increasing the number of its members, the CC, I think, must also, and perhaps mainly, devote attention to checking and improving our administrative machinery, which is no good at all. For this we must enlist the services of highly qualified specialists, and the task of supplying those special- ists must devolve upon the Workers' and Peasants' Inspection.

How are we to combine these checking specialists, people with adequate knowledge, and the new members of the CC? This problem must be resolved in practice.

It seems to me that the Workers' and Peasants' Inspection (as a result of its development and of our perplexity about its development) has led all in all to what we now observe, namely, to an intermediate position between a special People's Commissariat and a special function of the members of the CC; between an institution that inspects anything and everything and an aggregate of not very numerous but first- class inspectors, who must be well paid (this is especially indispensable in our age when everything must be paid for and inspectors are directly employed by the institutions that pay them better).

If the number of CC members is increased in the appro- priate way, and they go through a course of state management year after year with the help of highly qualified specialists and of members of the Workers' and Peasants' Inspection who are highly authoritative in every branch—then, I think, we shall successfully solve this problem, which we have not managed to do for such a long time.

To sum up, 100 members of the CC at the most and not more than 400–500 assistants, members of the Workers' and Peasants' Inspection, engaged in inspecting under their direction.

Lenin

December 29, 1922
Taken down by M.V.

*   *   *

Continuation of the notes.
December 30, 1922

THE QUESTION OF NATIONALITIES OR "AUTONOMIZATION"

I suppose I have been very remiss with respect to the workers of Russia for not having intervened energetically and decisively enough in the notorious question of autonomization, which, it appears, is officially called the question of the union of Soviet socialist republics.

When this question arose last summer, I was ill; and then in the autumn I relied too much on my recovery and on the October and December Plenums giving me an opportunity of intervening in this question. However, I did not manage to attend the October Plenum Meeting (when this question came up) or the one in December, and so the question passes me by almost completely.

I have only had time for a talk with Comrade Dzerzhinskií, who came from the Caucasus and told me how this matter stood in Georgia. I have also managed to exchange a few words with Comrade Zinovyev and express my apprehensions on this matter. From what I was told by Comrade Dzerzhinskií, who was at the head of the commission sent by the CC to "investigate" the Georgian incident, I could only draw the greatest apprehensions. If matters had come to such a pass that Ordzhonikidze could go to the extreme of applying physical violence, as Comrade Dzerzhinskií informed me, we can imaging what a mess we have got ourselves into. Obviously the whole business of "autonomization" was radically wrong and badly timed.

It is said that a united apparatus was needed. Where did that assurance come from? Did it not come from that same Russian apparatus which, as I pointed out in one of the preceding sections of my diary, we took over from tsarism and slightly anointed with Soviet oil?

There is no doubt that that measure should have been delayed somewhat until we could say that we vouched for our apparatus as our own. But now, we must, in all conscience, admit the contrary; the apparatus we call ours is, in fact, still quite alien to us; it is a bourgeois and tsarist hotch-potch and there has been no possibility of getting rid of it in the course of the past five years without the help of other countries and because we have been "busy" most of the time with military engagements and the fight against famine.

It is quite natural that in such circumstances the "freedom to secede from the union," by which we justify ourselves, will be a mere scrap of paper, unable to defend the non-Russians from the onslaught of that really Russian man, the Great-Russian chauvinist, in substance a rascal and a tyrant, such as the typical Russian bureaucrat is. There is no doubt that the infinitesimal percentage of Soviet and sovietized workers will drown in that tide of chauvinistic Great-Russian riffraff like a fly in milk.

It is said in defense of this measure that the People's Commissariats directly concerned with national psychology and national education were set up as separate bodies. But there the question arises: can these People's Commissariats be made quite independent? and secondly: were we careful enough to take measures to provide the non-Russians with a real safeguard against the truly Russian bully? I do not think we took such measures, although we could and should have done so.

I think Stalin's haste and his infatuation with pure administration, together with his spite against the notorious "nationalist-socialism," played a fatal role here. In politics, spite generally plays the basest of roles.

I also fear that Comrade Dzerzhinskií, who went to the Caucasus to investigate the "crime" of those "nationalist-socialists," distinguished himself there by his truly Russian frame of mind (it is common knowledge that people of other nationalities who have become Russified overdo this Russian frame of mind) and that the impartiality of his whole commission was typified well enough by Ordzhonikidze's "man-handling." I think that no provocation or even insult can justify Russian manhandling and that Comrade Dzerzhinskií was inexcusably guilty in adopting a light-hearted attitude toward it.

For all the citizens in the Caucasus, Ordzhonikidze was the authority. Ordzhonikidze had no right to display that irritability to which he and Dzerzhinskií referred. On the contrary, Ordzhonikidze should have behaved with a restraint that cannot be demanded of any ordinary citizen, still less of a man accused of a "political" crime. And, to tell the truth, those nationalist-socialists were citizens who were accused of a political crime, and the terms of the accusation were such that it could not be described otherwise.

Here we have an important question of principle: how is internationalism to be understood?[3]

Lenin

December 30, 1922
Taken down by M.V.

*   *   *

Continuation of the notes.
December 31, 1922

THE QUESTION OF NATIONALITIES
OR "AUTONOMIZATION"
(Continued)

In my writings on the national question I have already said that an abstract presentation of the question of nationalism in general is of no use at all. A distinction must necessarily be made between the nationalism of an oppressor nation and that of an oppressed nation, the nationalism of a big nation and that of a small nation.

In respect to the second kind of nationalism, we, nationals of a big nation, have nearly always been guilty, in historic practice, of an infinite number of cases of violence; furthermore, we commit violence and insult an infinite

---

3. After this, the following phrase was crossed out in the original: "It seems to me that our comrades have not studied this important question of principle sufficiently."

number of times without noticing it. It is sufficient to recall my Volga reminiscences of how non-Russians are treated; how the Poles are not called by any other name than Polyachishka, how the Tatar is nicknamed Prince, how the Ukrainians are always Khokhols, and the Georgians and other Caucasian nationals always Kapkasians.

That is why internationalism on the part of the oppressors or "great" nations, as they are called (though they are great only in their violence, only great as bullies), must consist not only in the observance of the formal equality of nations, but even in an inequality of the oppressor nation, the great nation, that must make up for the inequality that obtains in actual practice. Anybody who does not understand this has not grasped the real proletarian attitude to the national question; he is still essentially petit bourgeois in his point of view and is, therefore, sure to descend to the bourgeois point of view.

What is important for the proletarian? For the proletarian it is not only important, it is absolutely essential that he should be assured that the non-Russians place the greatest possible trust in the proletarian class struggle. What is needed to ensure this? Not merely formal equality. In one way or another, by one's attitude or by concessions, it is necessary to compensate the non-Russians for the lack of trust, for the suspicion and the insults to which the government of the "dominant" nation subjected them in the past.

I think it is unnecessary to explain this to Bolsheviks, to Communists, in greater detail. And I think that in the present instance, as far as the Georgian nation is concerned, we have a typical case in which a genuinely proletarian attitude makes profound caution, thoughtfulness, and a readiness to compromise a matter of necessity for us. The

Georgian who is neglectful of this aspect of the question, or who carelessly flings about accusations of "nationalist-socialism" (whereas he himself is a real and true "nationalist-socialist," and even a vulgar Great-Russian bully), violates, in substance, the interests of proletarian class solidarity, for nothing holds up the development and strengthening of proletarian class solidarity so much as national injustice; "offended" nationals are not sensitive to anything so much as to the feeling of equality and the violation of this equality, if only through negligence or jest—to the violation of that equality by their proletarian comrades. That is why in this case it is better to overdo rather than underdo the concessions and leniency toward the national minorities. That is why, in this case, the fundamental interest of proletarian solidarity, and consequently of the proletarian class struggle, requires that we never adopt a formal attitude to the national question, but always take into account the specific attitude of the proletarian of the oppressed (or small) nation towards the oppressor (or great) nation.

Lenin

Taken down by M.V.
December 31, 1922

*   *   *

Continuation of the notes.
December 31, 1922

What practical measures must be taken in the present situation?

Firstly, we must maintain and strengthen the union of socialist republics. Of this there can be no doubt. This measure is necessary for us and it is necessary for the world communist proletariat in its struggle against the world bourgeoisie and its defense against bourgeois intrigues.

Secondly, the union of socialist republics must be retained for its diplomatic apparatus. By the way, this apparatus is an exceptional component of our state apparatus. We have not allowed a single influential person from the old tsarist apparatus into it. All sections with any authority are composed of Communists. That is why it has already won for itself (this may be said boldly) the name of a reliable communist apparatus purged to an incomparably greater extent of the old tsarist, bourgeois, and petit bourgeois elements than that which we have had to make do with in other People's Commissariats.

Thirdly, exemplary punishment must be inflicted on Comrade Ordzhonikidze (I say this all the more regretfully as I am one of his personal friends and have worked with him abroad) and the investigation of all the material that Dzerzhinskii's commission has collected must be completed or started over again to correct the enormous mass of wrongs and biased judgments that it doubtlessly contains. The political responsibility for all this truly Great-Russian nationalist campaign must, of course, be laid on Stalin and Dzerzhinskii.

Fourthly, the strictest rules must be introduced on the use of the national language in the non-Russian republics of our union, and these rules must be checked with special care. There is no doubt that with our apparatus being what it is, there is bound to be, on the pretext of unity in the railway service, unity in the fiscal service, and so on, a mass of truly Russian abuses. Special ingenuity is necessary for the struggle against these abuses, not to mention special sincerity on the part of those who undertake this struggle.

A detailed code will be required, and only the nationals living in the republic in question can draw it up at all successfully. And then we cannot be sure in advance that as a result of this work we shall not take a step backward at our next Congress of Soviets, i.e., retain the union of Soviet socialist republics only for military and diplomatic affairs, and in all other respects restore full independence to the individual People's Commissariats.

It must be borne in mind that the decentralization of the People's Commissariats and the lack of coordination in their work as far as Moscow and other centers are concerned can be compensated sufficiently by Party authority, if it is exercised with sufficient prudence and impartiality; the harm that can result to our state from a lack of unification between the national apparatuses and the Russian apparatus is infinitely less than that which will be done not only to us, but to the whole International, and to the hundreds of millions of the peoples of Asia, which is destined to follow us on to the stage of history in the near future. It would be unpardonable opportunism if, on the eve of the debut of the East, just as it is awakening, we undermined our prestige with its peoples, even if only by the slightest crudity or injustice toward our own non-Russian nationalities. The need to rally against the imperialists of the West, who are defending the capitalist world, is one thing. There can be no doubt about that and it would be superfluous for me to speak about my unconditional approval of it. It is another thing when we ourselves lapse, even if only in trifles, into imperialist attitudes toward oppressed nationalities, thus undermining all our principled sincerity, all our principled defense of the struggle against imperialism. But the morrow of world history will be a day when the awakening peoples oppressed by imperialism are finally aroused and the decisive long and hard struggle for their liberation begins.

Lenin

December 31, 1922
Taken down by M.V.

*   *   *

HOW WE SHOULD REORGANIZE THE WORKERS' AND PEASANTS' INSPECTION
(RECOMMENDATION TO THE TWELFTH CONGRESS)

It is beyond question that the Workers' and Peasants' Inspection is an enormous difficulty for us, and that so far this difficulty has not been overcome. I think that the comrades who try to overcome the difficulty by denying that the Workers' and Peasants' Inspection is useful and necessary are wrong. But I do not deny that the problem presented by our state apparatus and the task of improving it is very difficult, that it is far from being solved, and is an extremely urgent one.

With the exception of the People's Commissariat of Foreign Affairs, our state apparatus is to a considerable extent a survival of the past and has undergone hardly any serious change. It has only been slightly touched up on the surface, but in all other respects it is a most typical relic of our old state machine. And so, to find a method of really renovating it, I think we ought to turn for experience to our Civil War.

How did we act in the more critical moments of the Civil War?

We concentrated our best Party forces in the Red Army;

we mobilized the best of our workers; we looked for new forces at the deepest roots of our dictatorship.

I am convinced we must go to the same source to find the means of reorganizing the Workers' and Peasants' Inspection. I recommend that our Twelfth Party Congress adopt the following plan of reorganization, based on some enlargement of our Central Control Commission.

The Plenums of the Central Committee of our Party are already revealing a tendency to develop into a kind of supreme Party conference. They take place, on the average, not more than once in two months, while the routine work is conducted, as we know, on behalf of the Central Committee by our Politburo, our Orgburo, our Secretariat, and so forth. I think we ought to follow the road we have thus taken to the end and definitely transform the Plenums of the Central Committee into supreme Party conferences convened once in two months jointly with the Central Control Commission. The Central Control Commission should be amalgamated with the main body of the reorganized Workers' and Peasants' Inspection on the following lines.

I propose that the Congress should elect 75 to 100 new members to the Central Control Commission. They should be workers and peasants, and they should go through the same Party screening as ordinary members of the Central Committee, because they are to enjoy the same rights as the members of the Central Committee.

On the other hand, the staff of the Workers' and Peasants' Inspection should be reduced to three or four hundred persons, specially screened for conscientiousness and knowledge of our state apparatus. They must also undergo a special test as regards their knowledge of the principles of scientific organization of labor in general, and of administrative work, office work, and so forth, in particular.

In my opinion, such an amalgamation of the Workers' and Peasants' Inspection with the Central Control Commission will be beneficial to both these institutions. On the one hand, the Workers' and Peasants' Inspection will thus obtain such high authority that it will certainly not be inferior to the People's Commissariat of Foreign Affairs. On the other hand, our Central Committee, together with the Central Control Commission, will definitely take the road of becoming a supreme Party conference, which in fact it has already taken, and along which it should proceed to the end so as to be able to fulfill its functions properly in two respects: in respect to *its own* methodical, expedient, and systematic organization and work, and in respect to maintaining contacts with the broad masses through the medium of the best of our workers and peasants.

I foresee an objection that, directly or indirectly, may come from those spheres that make our state apparatus antiquated, i.e., from those who urge that its present utterly impossible, indecently prerevolutionary form be preserved (incidentally, we now have an opportunity that rarely occurs in history of ascertaining the period necessary for bringing about radical social changes; we now see clearly *what* can be done in five years, and what requires much more time).

The objection I foresee is that the change I propose will lead to nothing but chaos. The members of the Central Control Commission will wander around all the institutions, not knowing where, why, or to whom to apply, causing disorganization everywhere and distracting employees from their routine work, etc., etc.

I think the malicious source of this objection is so obvious that it does not warrant a reply. It goes without saying that the Presidium of the Central Control Commission, the People's Commissar of the Workers' and Peasants' Inspection and his collegium (and also, in the proper cases, the Secretariat of our Central Committee) will have to put in years of persistent effort to get the Commissariat properly organized, and to get it to function smoothly in conjunction with the Central Control Commission. In my opinion, the People's Commissar of the Workers' and Peasants' Inspection, as well as the whole collegium, can (and should) remain and guide the work of the entire Workers' and Peasants' Inspection, including the work of all the members of the Central Control Commission who will be "placed under his command." The three or four hundred employees of the Workers' and Peasants' Inspection that are to remain, according to my plan, should, on the one hand, perform purely secretarial functions for the other members of the Workers' and Peasants' Inspection and for the supplementary members of the Central Control Commission; and, on the other hand, they should be highly skilled, specially screened, particularly reliable, and highly paid, so that they may be relieved of their present truly unhappy (to say the least) position of Workers' and Peasants' Inspection officials.

I am sure the reduction of the staff to the number I have indicated will greatly enhance the efficiency of the Workers' and Peasants' Inspection personnel and the quality of all its work, enabling the People's Commissar and the members of the collegium to concentrate their efforts entirely on organizing work and on systematically and steadily improving its efficiency, which is so absolutely essential for our workers' and peasants' government, and for our Soviet system.

On the other hand, I also think that the People's Commissar of the Workers' and Peasants' Inspection should work on partly amalgamating and partly coordinating those higher institutions for the organization of labor (the Central Institute of Labor, the Institute for the Scientific Organization of Labor, etc.), of which there are now no fewer than twelve in our Republic. Excessive uniformity and a consequent desire to amalgamate will be harmful. On the contrary, what is needed here is a reasonable and expedient mean between amalgamating all these institutions and properly delimiting them, allowing for a certain independence for each of them.

Our own Central Committee will undoubtedly gain no less from this reorganization than the Workers' and Peasants' Inspection. It will gain because its contacts with the masses will be greater and because the regularity and effectiveness of its work will improve. It will then be possible (and necessary) to institute a stricter and more responsible procedure of preparing for the meetings of the Politburo, which should be attended by a definite number of members of the Central Control Commission determined either for a definite period or by some organizational plan.

In distributing work to the members of the Central Control Commission, the People's Commissar of the Workers' and Peasants' Inspection, in conjunction with the Presidium of the Central Control Commission, should impose on them the duty either of attending the meetings of the Politburo for the purpose of examining all the documents appertaining to matters that come before it in one way or another; or of devoting their working time to theoretical study, to the study of scientific methods of organizing labor; or of taking a practical part in the work of supervising and improving our machinery of state, from the higher state institutions to the lower local bodies, etc.

I also think that in addition to the political advantages accruing from the fact that the members of the Central Committee and the Central Control Commission will, as a consequence of this reform, be much better informed and better prepared for the meetings of the Politburo (all the documents relevant to the business to be discussed at these meetings should be sent to all the members of the Central Committee and the Central Control Commission not later than the day before the meeting of the Politburo, except in absolutely urgent cases, for which special methods of informing the members of the Central Committee and the Central Control Commission and of settling these matters must be devised), there will also be the advantage that the influence of purely personal and incidental factors in our Central Committee will diminish, and this will reduce the danger of a split.

Our Central Committee has grown into a strictly centralized and highly authoritative group, but the conditions under which this group is working are not commensurate with its authority. The reform I recommend should help to remove this defect, and the members of the Central Control Commission, whose duty it will be to attend all meetings of the Politburo in a definite number, will have to form a compact group that should not allow anybody's authority without exception, neither that of the General Secretary nor of any other member of the Central Committee, to prevent them from putting questions, verifying documents, and, in general, from keeping themselves fully informed of all things and from exercising the strictest control over the proper conduct of affairs.

Of course, in our Soviet Republic, the social order is based on the collaboration of two classes: the workers and peasants, in which the "Nepmen," i.e., the bourgeoisie, are now permitted to participate on certain terms. If serious class disagreements arise between these classes, a split will be inevitable. But the grounds for such a split are not inevitable in our social system, and it is the principal task of our Central Committee and Central Control Commission, as well as of our Party as a whole, to watch very closely over such circumstances as may cause a split, and to forestall them; for in the final analysis the fate of our Republic will depend on whether the peasant masses will stand by the working class, loyal to their alliance, or whether they will permit the "Nepmen," i.e., the new bourgeoisie, to drive a wedge between them and the working class, to split them off from the working class. The more clearly we see this alternative, the more clearly all our workers and peasants understand it, the greater are the chances that we shall avoid a split, which would be fatal for the Soviet Republic.

January 23, 1923

*   *   *

[Publisher's note: *Please observe the salutations and closing remarks of the following two letters. It is interesting to see the difference in feeling expressed in this letter to Trotsky as compared to the note dictated on December 21, 1922. Also note the different attitudes that Lenin expresses toward Trotsky and Stalin on this day.]*

Top secret
Personal

Dear Comrade Trotsky:

It is my earnest request that you should undertake the defense of the Georgian case in the Party CC. This case is now under "persecution" by Stalin and Dzerzhinskii, and I cannot rely on their impartiality. Quite the contrary. I would feel at ease if you agreed to undertake its defense. If you should refuse to do so for any reason, return the whole case to me. I shall consider it a sign that you do not accept.

With best comradely greetings,
Lenin

Dictated by phone
on March 5, 1923

*   *   *

Top secret
Personal

Copy to Comrades Kamenev and Zinovyev

Dear Comrade Stalin:

You have been so rude as to summon my wife to the telephone and use bad language. Although she had told you that she was prepared to forget this, the fact nevertheless became known through her to Zinovyev and Kamenev. I have no intention of forgetting so easily what has been done against me, and it goes without saying that what has been done against my wife I consider having been done against me as well. I ask you, therefore, to think over whether you are prepared to withdraw what you have said and to make your apologies, or whether you prefer that relations between us should be broken off.

Respectfully yours,
Lenin

March 5, 1923

*   *   *

Comrades Mdivani, Makharadze, and others
Copy to Comrades *Trotsky and Kamenev*

Dear Comrades:

I am following your case with all my heart. I am indignant over Ordzhonikidze's rudeness and the connivance of Stalin and Dzerzhinskií. I am preparing for you notes and a speech.

Respectfully yours,
Lenin

March 6, 1923[4]

The above dictations are reprinted from V.I. Lenin, *Collected Works, Volume 33* (Moscow: Progress Publishers, 1966), pp. 481–486; *Collected Works, Volume 36* (Moscow: Progress Publishers, 1966), pp. 594–611; and *Collected Works, Volume 45* (Moscow: Progress Publishers, 1970), pp. 606–608.

---

4. This is the last dictation that Lenin made. Four days later he suffered a stroke that left him incapable of speech.

Yuri A. Buranov is a professor of history and head of the Department of Research and Publication at the Russian Center for the Preservation and Study of Modern History Documents (the former Central Party Archives), Moscow. His fields of professional interest are the economic and political aspects of the history of post-reform Russia (1861–1917). He is the author of *Privatization of the Urals Mining and Metallurgical Industry* (1982); and coauthor, with Vladimir M. Khrustalev (Chrustaljow), of *Fall of the Imperial Home* (1992) and *Die Zaren-Mörder: Vernichtung einer Dynastie* (1993). He is also a contributor to *A History of the Urals*, vol. 2 (1990).